HOW TO BUY A HOUSE FOR A DOLLAR

RICK OTTON

HOW TO BUY A HOUSE FOR A DOLLAR

www.howtobuyahouseforadollar.com

This edition first printed 2011

Disclaimer

Australian National Library Cataloguing-in-Publication Entry

Otton, Rick, with Jade Barclay
How to buy a house for a dollar
First Edition
ISBN: 978-0-646-51892-3 (pbk)
Subjects: House buying - Finance. Real Estate investment. Finance, personal.
Dewey Number: 643.12

Published in Australia by We Buy Houses Pty Ltd
Edited by Kerrin Medenyak
Typesetting and layout by Bookhouse, Sydney (www.bookhouse.com.au)
Printed and bound in Australia by McPherson's Printing Group

Distributed in Australia by We Buy Houses Pty Ltd

ACKNOWLEDGEMENTS

Thank you to my students in Australia, New Zealand, the United Kingdom and around the world who are my daily inspiration and the reason I wrote this book.

A big thank you to the team who helped me put this book together: Jade Barclay, Dale Beaumont, Kerrin Medenyak, and Simon Paterson.

Thank you to my team at We Buy Houses and Rickotton.com: Katrina Barkworth, Lisa Gordon, Mark Jones, Jackie Layoun, Phillip Parisis, Lauren Thomas, and Mawar Aras. I appreciate your efforts, and thanks for making me look good!

Thank you to my family and friends who continue to love and support me through the continual evolution of my business-building.

Thank you Allan Pease, my first mentor, for employing me over 30 years ago and showing me that anything is possible.

To the folks at the Outback Pub in Dallas, Texas – thanks for feeling sorry for me and offering me a job. Otherwise, I would never have stayed long enough in the USA to experience the Savings and Loans crisis in early 1990s, which started me on my journey buying houses for a dollar in order to avoid a career at McDonald's.

Thanks also to the people of the USA for continuously motivating me with their 'can do' spirit.

Thanks David Lee for convincing me to show the United Kingdom how to 'buy houses for a pound'.

I'm very thankful for the valued friendship and wise counsel of my solicitor, Anthony Cordato, who, for over a decade, has helped me find a way to transform my entrepreneurial property ideas into action.

Thank you to my great friend and mentor, Rick Manietta who listened and believed in my 'out of the square' business plan, who helped me launch We Buy Houses over a decade ago and who still continues to kick my butt and inspire me today!

Finally, thank you to Jane Otton for believing in me and seeing my potential long before I did.

I dedicate this book to all property buyers and sellers in the world who are frustrated with the current system of buying and selling property the traditional way. You continue to motivate me to find solutions to help solve your problems so you can achieve your dreams.

RICK OTTON

To Christina
Success in activity
repeated

CONTENTS

ALL ABOUT BUYING

ALL ABOUT SELLING

FIVE CORE STRATEGIES

FOREWORD

BY DALE BEAUMONT

I first met Rick Otton back in 2005 when I attended a real estate seminar. Sitting in my chair, I was mesmerised by Rick's unorthodox yet effective way of buying houses.

Inspired by what I learnt, I decided to write a book titled *Secrets of Property Millionaires Exposed*. As it was my desire to expose people to real-life success stories, I invited Rick to be part of the book and was delighted when he said yes. That book has since gone on to be a national bestseller.

That was a number of years ago and during that time I've often said: 'Rick your strategies are amazing. You really need to write your own book'. Well, after a lot of time and effort, that book is finally here.

Having had a chance to get to know Rick personally I can say he's the real deal. He has used these strategies for over 20 years to amass a property portfolio worth millions. But to do something yourself is one thing; to be able to teach others how to replicate your success is completely different.

In the last decade Rick has put his ideas to the ultimate test by teaching his formula to those ready to listen and apply themselves. As a result, today there are literally thousands of success stories from his students, some of which you'll read about in this book.

But in order to embrace Rick's ideas, you are going to need to open your mind.

People who think like entrepreneurs are open to embracing change. They are flexible and forward thinking. They recognise the opportunity for change. And they seize that opportunity; they tackle it, make it more efficient, and before long it becomes the new standard.

On a final note, I want to encourage you to take the next step after reading this book. It is great to be motivated and get some ideas. But knowledge is not power. It is the application of that knowledge which is key. And to support you with that process Rick and his team have a number of additional resources to offer you. So head to Rick's website and keep moving forward.

Now, enjoy reading this book and have fun building your wealth!

Dale Beaumont
Creator of the Secrets Exposed Series
Author of 16 best-selling books

PREFACE

CAN YOU REALLY BUY A HOUSE FOR A DOLLAR?

Yes, you can! And I'm here to show you how. Along with my students in Australia, New Zealand and the United Kingdom, I'm living proof that you can buy property every day for a dollar or a pound, and in this book, we'll show you how. You'll meet some of my students, and they'll share their case studies and stories with you so you can see for yourself how it's done.

I hope this book challenges some of your commonly held views about property investing. I wrote this to open your mind, so you can see ways to transact property other than the system most people currently use.

It is my belief that some aspects of the traditional property system are dated and no longer work for either buyers or sellers. The strategies I lay out in this book can solve current property problems such as:

How to fulfil your dream of home ownership even when our property prices are some of the highest in the world

Recently, US economist Harry Dent said from stage that Sydney house prices are the highest in the world after Vancouver. These high property prices are making it increasingly difficult for first-time homebuyers to save for their deposit and stamp duty. Many adults in their 20s and 30s are concerned they may be permanently locked out of the housing market, and never achieve their dream of home ownership.

How to buy property without qualifying for a bank loan

Since banks have pulled back on lending money due to the Global Financial Crisis, it's become more difficult to qualify for, and receive, a bank loan. And now a buyer needs to save even more money for a deposit! In turn, this makes it more challenging for sellers to achieve their asking price, it takes longer to sell property, and it creates added uncertainty about whether buyers can even qualify for loans.

How to turn an existing negatively geared property into a cash flow positive or neutral one

Australia is one of only three countries in the world that structure negative gearing the way we do; the other two are Canada and New Zealand. While I believe negative gearing has a place in a property investment portfolio, there are a large number of investors and home owners who are now finding it difficult to make their mortgage payments on negatively geared properties, for a variety of different reasons – which is why they need to generate cash flow.

The good news is each of these problems can be solved!

You'll find the solutions laid out inside this book. As well as learning the ins and outs of transacting property without applying for a bank loan or saving a large deposit and stamp duty, you'll discover that the secret to successfully investing in property is working together to find a unified way to solve today's property problems.

For two decades, I've been investing in property in multiple countries. I've learnt most people don't want to be millionaires; instead they want to experience the benefits that come from what money can buy. I'm not in love with any of my properties, but I do love the benefits that come from owning and controlling property.

In this book, I'll show you how to capture the benefits of property now and why this is the new way forward, even if you've never invested in property. And if you're a seasoned investor or own your own home you'll still be surprised by what you'll discover. You may desire an income stream from property, or to make positive cash flow in a capital city without buying investment properties in a mining town or the outback, or to build long-term wealth. In this book you'll find an idea or specific strategy that has potential to transform the way you think and invest for the rest of your life.

Rick Otton
Sydney, Australia

Imagine ...

Imagine buying a house without a bank.

Imagine buying your home using none of your own money.

Imagine buying a house even with less-than-perfect credit ...

... without paying stamp duty.

... without borrowing equity from your existing property.

... without saving for a deposit!

I'm Rick Otton, and in this book I'll show you that it's possible.

I t is possible to buy property using little, or none, of your own money. It is possible to become a property entrepreneur even if you've never bought or sold a house in your life. And it's possible for both the buyer and the seller to get what they want at the same time. It's not only possible, thousands of people from all walks of life have been doing it for years. And if they can do it, you can do it too.

Thousands of people throughout Australia and New Zealand are already buying and selling property the easy way, but there are still many people doing it the hard way. I'm here to show you that there is an easier way – in fact, by the time you've finished reading this book, you'll see that there are *many* easier ways.

I'll show you how you can buy your first home, grow your wealth with property and solve your property problems, without the headaches and hassles that have become so commonplace for most Australians and New Zealanders. And the best bit is that you don't need a lot of money or a bank loan to start using these strategies – just the willingness to see things a little differently.

THE PROFIT IS IN THE TERMS, NOT THE PRICE

In traditional price-led negotiations, where sellers want the price high and buyers want the price low, nobody wins except for the agents, banks and solicitors. The strategies I've discovered and developed over the past two decades take the focus off the price, and put it on flexible and convenient payment terms. This is how I can structure transactions where the buyer AND the seller both get what they really want.

I learnt early on that there are five things that go up in value over time, and property is one of them. I've always felt more comfortable investing in houses than anything else because they make sense – everybody needs one, and they don't disappear overnight like shares can. Despite recent financial turmoil, property is still great to invest in, even though the banks have made loans harder to get. What's stopping people from investing in property now is qualifying for bank loans. But if we come up with ways to remove the obstacle of saving a deposit or getting a bank loan, property is still the greatest way to build wealth.

It's all about changing processes

People say that I'm a property guy, or that I'm the creative finance guy. But really I'm a process guy. I look at processes that have been accepted and unchanged for a long time, and I ask:

> 'Is this the best way? Or is it just a hand-me-down process that no one ever changed?'

> 'Is this the most efficient process?'

> 'Just suppose we did it another way ...'

I apply this way of thinking and changing processes to everything, and I recommend that my students do too. I'm most passionate about changing processes with property transactions because property affects everyone. It's such a big part of our lives. Whenever I change part of the process of buying and selling property, it unlocks hidden opportunities for people, solves problems that old processes simply couldn't solve, and has ripple effects that can help so many people and improve so many lives.

OPTIONAL HASSLES

When selling a property, most people accept the following hassles as an unavoidable part of the process:

- being charged high fees by agents and advertisers
- having the house on the market for a long time

- not knowing whether anyone will show up for an open house
- being pushed to drop the price when agents can't sell
- market fluctuations making it harder to sell.

Similarly, most buyers accept the following hassles as unavoidable:

- paying stamp duty and legal fees
- saving up for a traditional 10% or 20% deposit
- qualifying for a bank loan
- dealing with real estate agents.

However, all of these hassles are entirely optional. Most of my students have completed transactions that avoid some or all of them. In fact, my students find that it's much more common for them to:

- sell a house in an hour, a day or a week
- avoid agent commissions and advertising fees
- not need a traditional deposit – buyers just move in and start making payments
- get the sale price they want fast, in any market.

Everything's optional, and everything's flexible. Once you accept this as a principle and fact of life, everything will change for you. Questioning convention and creating new processes are valuable skills – especially today, when the pace of change is faster than anyone could have dreamed of just a few short decades ago.

Traditional processes often create problems. But I'm into solving problems, and creating processes that solve problems by default. I'm always finding easier and more efficient ways of doing things. I'm always asking, 'Why does it have to be hard?' The answer is: 'It doesn't. It can be easy. There's *always* an easier way'.

WE DON'T HAVE TO BE TOLD WHAT TO DO

Let's say two guys meet at the side of the road. One has a sixpack of soft drinks and the other has a pizza. They start talking and decide to swap the soft drinks for the pizza. Nobody thinks anything of it. They agree, they swap and they're both happy. It's no big deal. It's simple and easy.

But if you change that same simple swap from food to houses, it suddenly seems a lot harder. The truth is that it's no different at all, but when houses are involved we've learnt to make it more difficult – for ourselves and for everyone else.

There is *always* more than one way to skin a cat. Most of the time you won't be told the most efficient way to do things – usually you're told the most commonly used way, or the traditional way, which hasn't been improved or made any more efficient for a few hundred years. The conventional processes usually just make things easier for solicitors (because they don't have to think of anything new, they just photocopy a form) and make things unnecessarily complicated and expensive for buyers and sellers.

Here's what I believe, and I've seen it work in practice thousands of times: if two people want to transfer an item or two between them, those two people should be able to agree over a coffee or an ice-cream, and come to a simple arrangement that works for them both.

Farmers used to do it all the time before banks got involved, swapping sheep and grain for pieces of land, or paying instalments over a number of years instead of paying the full amount up-front. They were flexible. They were open to different ideas. They talked to each other. And when it was obvious that the usual process wasn't going to solve their problems, or before a 'standard process' had been invented and accepted far and wide, they thought things through. They talked one on one and created a new process that worked.

Creative financing is all about creating processes that solve problems. If you're going to solve someone's problems in the terms of a transaction, you need the whole story. Going direct, talking one on one like the farmers did, with the buyer talking directly to the seller, is part of making these strategies work.

Over the years I've done the same thing with houses in America, Australia, New Zealand and the United Kingdom. Not long after I started, people were asking my wife and me how we did what we were doing. There are no secrets, and there is more than enough opportunity for everybody, so we started showing people exactly how we see and do things differently so that they could start to do it themselves. First we taught a few friends, then more and more people. Our purpose has grown from creating time and financial freedom for ourselves to being able to help as many people as we can to see things differently and create their own freedom.

The strategies we're revealing in this book are all duplicable and transferable. They've changed not only our lives, but thousands of our students' lives as well, and you'll see actual examples of our students putting real-life transactions together that solve real-life problems, including:

- buying without a bank loan
- turning negative gearing around to positive cash flow
- selling when the mortgage is worth more than the house, without needing to write a cheque to cover the difference
- creating stepping stones to help everyday people get into home ownership
- profiting from renovations without lifting a finger.

Literally thousands of students have used our strategies (the exact same strategies you're about to learn in the following pages) to turn their lives around. Our students have been changing lives and creating financial freedom for themselves and their families, and impacting dozens, and sometimes hundreds, of other people's lives in the process.

You're about to learn how to build your own property portfolio from scratch using none of your own money, and why we believe absolutely anyone, regardless of their background or circumstances – anyone who truly wants a better life, and is willing to step outside the square and see things and do things a little differently – can do the same.

FINDING PROPERTY BUYERS MADE EASY CHECKLIST

(Value $17.95 – yours FREE)

How do you know if a potential buyer is qualified for you to finance? Download this simple checklist and find out with a few simple questions.

Download your **FREE Finding Property Buyers Made Easy Checklist** here:

www.howtobuyahouseforadollar.com/free-stuff

2

An easier way

What if you could buy as many houses as you wanted, using little or none of your own money and without getting a bank loan (even if you have less-than-perfect credit or have been locked out of the traditional banking system)? How many would you buy and how fast would you buy them?

What if you could sell houses quickly, within a week or less, and get access to the cash locked up in the houses without delay?

What if you could make a living by making other people's lives easier, by solving seemingly unsolvable financial problems simply by transferring houses from people who no longer want them to people who do?

I started buying and selling houses in the US in 1991, from scratch, without a cent to my name, at a time of financial mayhem when all the banks had stopped giving out loans in response to the Savings and Loans crisis. Within 12 months Jane and I:

- bought 76 apartments and houses
- made over $20,000 per month in positive cash flow
- made our money for the week by 9.30 am each day.

These days I spend most of my time onstage, travelling the world or working with my mentoring students, presenting seminars to help people just like you create all the time, location (which we'll explain more in Chapter 8) and financial freedom they desire by buying and selling houses for a dollar.

One of the most important aspects of our business is the success of our students. Many of our students regularly make six-figure incomes in the house business. And a lot of them say the same thing (which was true for us as well) – 'We got into houses because of the money. But we kept doing it because every transaction feels so good, because we're helping people solve their problems. Helping people out in this way isn't just profitable, it feels amazing! The feeling is awesome! Every time I do a transaction, I get to help more people, and this is the key not only to success, but to lasting fulfilment and happiness'.

In this book you'll discover how you can start buying and selling houses today, from scratch, and start to profit instantly – even if you have:

- never owned a house
- never saved a deposit
- less-than-perfect credit.

You will discover a range of possibilities, as we take you through some of the proven and successful processes that we use ourselves to make money with houses.

Millions of people want to buy or sell a house at any moment in time, and are having trouble achieving that dream using traditional methods. You could exponentially increase your income by helping these people to get what they want – and maybe become the next property millionaire in the process!

Every day, across Australia and New Zealand, there are people doing just that, just by doing one or two things differently. These everyday people have purchased their first home, have bought back their freedom, are spending all the time they want with their families, and are now living life entirely on their own terms. And they are everyday people just like you. If you're not one of them, you NEED this book – now more than ever.

RECLAIM YOUR FREEDOM

For years we've been trying to solve new problems with old systems. The fact of the matter is that traditional systems are falling apart all around us – they may have gotten us this far, but they never really worked that well in the first place. And no matter how good or bad things are with your personal situation, there's *never* been a better time to start using some more efficient systems.

The only difference between the people who have reclaimed their freedom and you is that those people have already discovered more efficient systems and better ways to buy and sell houses. And they have decided to do something about it. Now it's your turn to make that decision.

Are you fed up with your financial stresses and struggles forcing you to ...

drag yourself out of bed each day ...

to put on a suit or a uniform you don't need ...

to impress people you don't like ...

at a job you have no passion for ...

just so you can scrape through to next week and do it all again?

Or perhaps you're your own boss. Perhaps you got into business to be the master of your own destiny and have more time to spend with your family or doing the things you truly love. Has it really worked out that way, or ...

have you ended up a slave to your business instead ...

working more hours than you ever did in a job for half the pay (or less) ...

pushing yourself to the point of burnout ...

putting in all that effort to pay never-ending overheads, taxes, staff and suppliers ...

often not having anything left to pay yourself at the end of the month ...

and feeling like you'd be better off flipping burgers, because at least you'd get holiday and sick leave?

Can you remember the last time you woke up and felt genuinely excited about the day you were about to step into? How would your day, and your life, be different to how it is today if you had the cash, time and location freedom to be able to do what you truly enjoy, instead of having just enough to make it through the week?

Maybe you already have plenty of money, but no time to enjoy it. The truth is that you're not truly rich unless you have plenty of cash *and* plenty of time. Imagine if you could do what you want, when you want, with whomever you want, wherever you want, and you didn't have to worry about the daily grind. Imagine if you could stop working right now and be spontaneous, but the cash still kept rolling in. Even if you just replaced your current income, what kind of a difference would it make to your life and your family?

Imagine if every weekend was a long weekend. Imagine if the days and weeks stopped blending together, and you actually lived your life fully, instead of letting it pass you by, one hectic day at a time.

When you truly start to experience the power of seeing things a little differently, and buying and selling houses differently, with more efficient systems, you'll be able to put yourself into a whole new picture.

Imagine this ...

You leap out of bed on Monday morning, and every morning, excited about the day ahead. You feel refreshed and alive, and have time to have a leisurely breakfast with people you love at the coffee shop.

You meet with a homeowner at the coffee shop and help her find a way to sell her house fast before it goes into foreclosure. Then you meet up with a lovely couple who haven't been able to get a bank loan because they just moved here from overseas, and you help them get into a home for their family.

Maybe you're the only dad picking up your kids from school each day and playing at the park because you have the freedom that the other dads only dream about because they work nine-to-five jobs. You now work part-time, and it doesn't even feel like work. You have time to smell the roses, and you now make more money in a month than you used to make in a year.

At the end of another productive and fulfilling day, a wave of peace and gratitude washes over you, because you feel you are the master of your own destiny, and you have absolute certainty that you have the key to making cash on demand by helping people get what they truly want. You have the lifestyle you've always dreamed of, and the freedom to enjoy it, and you know for certain that you'll never have to worry about money ever again.

How would that make you feel?

Wouldn't it feel great? Of course it would – and if more people felt that way, the world would be a better place for us all to live in. And it's not the feelings that elude us. It's the systems that we use to do things that prevent us from feeling that way all the time.

That's one of the main reasons why I'm on a personal mission to transform the way people buy and sell property in Australia and New Zealand. I've already changed the way thousands of people buy and sell property over the last 20 years, but now I want to change the way the *majority* of people buy and sell their houses in these two countries.

Or at least make people aware that there is another way – a more efficient and profitable way. A way that means that buyers and sellers both get what they really want. But to do that, people need to start to change the way they see things first.

That's where this book comes in.

When you read this book, I want to get you to do three things:

- Start to see things differently.

- Be willing to change processes.

- 'Get' that the profit is in the terms, not the price.

Once you do that, you'll see a whole new world of possibility and opportunity open up in front of you. Then, as a bonus, I want you to do something with what you've learnt ... whether you buy a house yourself with no money, generate a decent retirement income, or help find a buyer for someone who has had their property on the market the traditional way for months and months and months. *Just do something new!*

And if you enjoy it, feel free to do it again ... and again ... and again.

YOU NEED TO KNOW 'WHY' IN ORDER TO SOLVE PEOPLE'S PROBLEMS

At any point in time, lots of people want to buy houses and lots of people want to sell houses – for all sorts of different reasons. You need to know *why* the seller is selling and *why* the buyer wants to buy. You need to know what the seller is trying to achieve – and that's often not actually about the money. It's about the problem that the money will solve. And you need to understand why the buyer wants to buy, and why they haven't been able to so far. Once you know the 'why', the rest is easy.

Here's what has been happening in Australia and New Zealand. Years ago, we all bought into the systems of negative gearing and growing wealth through property. When I started out I was told that when I bought enough houses I could eventually leave my job. The problem is that the more houses I bought that way, the more I needed the job. It seemed to me that I was pulling the plough so the banks could reap the harvest. When I spoke to my accountant, he said that the advantage of negative gearing was that if I lost enough money today, I could eventually make a profit someday. But it didn't make any sense to me.

Now the shortfalls of these systems are coming out. We need a plan B. We need a more efficient system.

We need to start to look at the process of buying and selling property, see what needs to be changed to solve the current problems, and then do it differently. Because this isn't really about property when you get down to it. It's about process.

It's about creating systems, methods and processes that benefit the other person first.

According to the Australian Bureau of Statistics (ABS) 1988-1989 Housing Survey, 70% of people who buy an investment property sell it within five years, because it's not giving them what they want it to give them. For a buy-and-hold strategy to grow some wealth, you usually need to hold for more than five years, but the vast majority of people don't. Or can't afford to.

The ABS also says 47% of people who sell within five years will either lose money or barely break even. So that 'buy and hold' thing really isn't doing what it promised.

Australians pay proportionally more for their homes than people in many other countries. While we may not buy our own home for purely financial reasons, anyone who buys an investment property buys it to *make* money. But that's not what's happening for most people – not by a long shot.

The financial stress of losing money as a result of holding onto unprofitable property also leads to a whole slew of other things we don't want:

- working more hours to make the mortgage payments
- emotional and physical stress
- poor health
- less time with family
- relationship breakdown.

These are all things we don't want.

It seems like the current system creates more problems than it solves. And even when we sell up and get out, in most cases that still doesn't solve the problem. It might reduce the burden a little, but we're often still left with a debt.

In his definitive book on the psychology of influence and persuasion, Robert Cialdini's research shows that there are six subconscious triggers of influence, and that the most powerful of all is reciprocity: the power of give and take.

Here's how I tap into Cialdini's Law of Reciprocity whenever I do a property transaction: if I give the buyer what he wants, and the seller what she wants, they are then compelled to give me what *I* want as well.

Just suppose we could create a better system ... a system that automatically solves problems, instead of one that automatically creates them.

Just suppose we could create a better system ... a more efficient system. Just suppose we could create processes that meant that we got what *we* want from the transaction, and so did the other person. Imagine a system that enabled you to get what you want, and left some profit in the property for the next person. Wouldn't that be better?

That's exactly what this book is all about.

In the following pages you'll find everything you need to start to see things differently, and you'll realise once and for all what the super-wealthy have known for lifetimes ... with the right vision, processes and paperwork, creating wealth is simple.

Let's get started!

3

That was then, this is now

It would be so nice if something
made sense for a change.

– Lewis Carroll, *Alice in Wonderland*

Standards are just the most accepted ways of doing things. They're usually not questioned, not challenged, not the most efficient, and not the best way of doing things. They're just the most commonly accepted way of doing things. And once something's accepted, people don't think about it anymore.

Before we had DVDs, TiVo and Blu-Ray, we had videos. There were two formats: Beta and VHS. Now, the better technology of the two

New formats will eventually become an accepted industry standard.

was Beta. But which one won in the end? That's right, VHS. Before DVDs took over, the only tapes that were still available were VHS tapes.

Now, VHS wasn't the best technology, but it was better than Beta in one way. Marketing. One company put out Beta. A conglomerate of lots of companies put out VHS, and they flooded the market. Soon there were many, many more videos available in VHS format. The product became cheaper, and more people bought it, and because people could afford to buy it, *VHS became the accepted industry standard*.

The same thing happened more recently with mp3 players. Various brands of mp3 players existed before Apple released the iPod, but Apple did something the other mp3 player manufacturers didn't. It made it easy and convenient for people to *access* their favourite music. Because iTunes became the accepted industry standard for downloading and managing music, iPods became the accepted industry standard for playing music on the run.

People want things to be easy – like iTunes makes music easy. Imagine if real estate was easy! Old thinking gets in the way of seeing new solutions, and we've just learnt that you can create new solutions that solve a lot of problems. Just suppose there was a paperwork system to support these new ideas.

It's all about solving the problem first and creating the paperwork second. Standard paperwork can be created to support any transaction – the paperwork is the glue that holds the transaction together.

I've been asked by students, 'Can someone agree to the sale of land over a kitchen table?' My solicitors have confirmed that there have been no oral contracts since the introduction of the Statute of Frauds in England in 1677. Since then, all contracts have had to be in writing and signed. But, as long as it's in writing, a 'heads of agreement' can be written and signed on a napkin, and be sufficient until a formal contract is written and signed.

WHAT'S THE STANDARD?

What made the current standard contract standard in the first place? Some guy with a pen wrote the basics down in 1919, and called it standard, and its use over time *made* it the standard. Someone created a form about 100 years ago and once people started using it, it became the accepted standard. Sure, it gets updated every so often, but the standard doesn't change!

People resist change because they're being told what to do by a quiet voice in the back of their mind. Resistance to changing to a better standard comes from one place – it's all because of scripts and old adopted processes.

Scripts are handed-down ways of doing things that become habits. They live in the back bit of our brains, interfering with, and protesting against, anything new we ever try to do. Scripts generally get us through the day without having to ask awkward questions or think very much. But they don't get us what we want or make us more efficient.

I'm not sure if your grandmother does this, but my grandmother always turned the teapot three times before pouring tea. She refused to drink tea out of an unturned pot. She had always done it that way, and always would. She insisted that the tea tasted better from a turned pot. That was her script.

When I was going out years ago, my father would say, 'Son, let me show you the short cuts'. And he'd describe this convoluted way to get where I was going, through all the backstreets that had been there since before the war. I'd say, 'Dad, there's a freeway there now'. But he wouldn't have a bar of the 'newfangled' freeway. His way was handed down and burnt in, and he'd never change it. And that was his script.

A new and better standard

We're always creating new paperwork systems to support new ideas – we just call it the 'standard form', and people adopt it quickly.

We've started to change the standards. And on the rare occasion that people baulk at it, we simply say, 'Oh, you're just working with the old standard. This is the new standard'. And they're happy with that.

I was with a solicitor the other day, doing a legal document. There were hundreds of pages in this option document and I asked the solicitor why we need all that. He said we don't need hardly any of it; it's just easier to copy the standard precedent. That's what solicitors call existing paperwork systems – precedents. So, we could reduce 70% of the paperwork, but finding out which 70% is no longer necessary would be expensive and take time.

And who's going to pay for it to be done? Who's going to stop long enough to change it?

Old paperwork systems from the 1900s have contingencies for every mishap that might happen once in a blue moon. Sixty-page contracts for commercial property are used for residential property when we don't need any more than a fraction of it. But it's easier for the solicitors to just copy the whole thing than to sift out the bits we need and create a shorter contract that only includes what we need for today's transactions.

We're using paperwork systems that have been handed down and handed down by solicitors for years and years and years. And they've *never* been made any more efficient.

More efficient paperwork systems work. Buyers and sellers want them. Solicitors want them, but they don't want to have to take the time to change the paperwork themselves. They just want to photocopy the old stuff because that's easier and quicker than making it more efficient.

The standard is whatever gets used the most by the most people. You can create a standard form with a pen, just as easily as that guy did in 1919. And when more and more people start using your form, it naturally becomes the new standard.

You CAN change the terms to suit whatever you agree to.

If people can no longer afford to do things the old way, they'll *have* to stop doing things that way. And they'll look for a new way that they can afford – even if it's a way that some guy with a pen creates (even if *you* create it). If people can afford it and it's a better way, it'll become the new accepted industry standard.

Paperwork can be written to legally support any transaction you create. But you don't have to start from scratch. Just have the right numbers on speed dial on your phone to get the paperwork done that will support your transactions and your ideas. To speed up the process, we actually give all our students copies of the standard paperwork we use for all the most common processes. And they meet the solicitors who put legal paperwork together. So you can give our legal paperwork to your own solicitors, and if they have any questions, they can call our guy and straighten out the details in 'legalese'.

4

Starting from scratch

HOW I LEARNT ABOUT VENDOR FINANCE

This story isn't just about me. It's just as much about my wife, Jane. Jane is from the USA and I'm from Australia. Jane was the one who showed me that Americans don't invest in property. Americans grow up familiar with investing in stocks and bonds; Australians grow up familiar and comfortable with investing in bricks and mortar.

The real turning point that got me into buying and selling houses was meeting Jane. We first met in 1990 at a party in Dallas – it was a 'Meet the Aussie' party and I was the guest of honour. We instantly connected, but then I had to come back to Australia. We talked for hours every day. Everyone said we weren't going to stay together because it was just one of those 'shipboard' romances. But we didn't care what they said, and we stayed connected.

I was selling insurance part-time when we met, I'd been travelling a lot and I was living with my parents. As Jane says, I did not look good on paper! Any outsider who looked at me would have seen a 34-year-old guy who still lived with his parents, worked part-time, and had no money ... and that's the guy who Jane met, fell in love with and married!

We were both very creative, and we believed that anything was possible. That was what was most attractive to both of us. As Jane says, we were creative souls and we had a mutual meeting of the minds. We both wanted to build something amazing together – but we had no idea what it was. Within a year of meeting we got married (because we couldn't afford the phone bills anymore!). We met in September 1990, and we got married in August 1991.

Before I met Jane I had lived and worked in New York and various other places around the world, but I always needed to go home to Australia whenever I ran out of money. I had a little, beat-up $200 Peugeot and I was so broke I had to tear the windscreen wipers off so I wouldn't get parking tickets. I lost every kind of job you can think of. I tried serving eggs in the Hamptons. I was a gardener in London, but I accidentally tore down a fence with my truck, so they let me go. I drove a double-decker tour bus for a while in Europe and I created a small oil slick around the Colosseum, so they let me go, too. I worked in a chocolate shop and sold chocolates; I sold those little security tags on clothes that beep when you leave the store; I was a meat salesman in Denver. I got five dollars an hour for putting hot-tar roofs on houses in Florida – I had to staple-gun linoleum tiles onto the roof, and you're meant to put them on straight so they don't leak. Well ... they let me go as well.

When we got married I had no university education, no qualifications, no savings and no job – Jane had a mid-level job in advertising. We had no money at all between us and we were living in a rented apartment. We were

We knew our freedom would never be delivered by a job.

fond of saying that our backs were against the wall, so we couldn't go backward! We were already broke, and we had to move forward in our thinking and actions. Jane gave me a year to get my act together and make some money. This was the clincher – she said she would support me for one year and then I had to get a job, even if it was just for seven bucks an hour. We always laugh about that now when we share it with our students. We realised that I was going to have to do *something* for a living, but the question was *what*.

We started brainstorming and we came up with a few ideas, but nothing that really clicked. So, we sat down and made a list of what was important to us.

We knew we loved to travel. We wanted time freedom; we didn't want to be tied down to nine-to-five hours. And we wanted the geographical freedom to be able to travel around the world, stay in close contact with both our families, and still have our money come in, wherever we were in the world. So whatever we did for money had to deliver that.

Even the best-paid job in the world still wouldn't give us the time and flexibility to travel and live the life we really wanted.

About that time, I noticed that houses in America were really, REALLY cheap. Too cheap. So I started investigating and researching it, and I realised that the American system was vastly different to the Australian one.

I'd bought houses before in Australia, but I didn't know what I was doing. I had just followed what everyone else was doing. I bought the houses with bank loans, just like everybody else, and they were all negatively geared. I had no idea how to build wealth or cash flow with houses – or how to buy them with no money.

I knew that property would be a good vehicle to make some money. I just hadn't figured out how yet. But I could smell a great opportunity because all the houses were so very cheap. I didn't know how to buy property, but I thought if it was THAT cheap, there had to be a way to make a few bucks out of it. I knew that somehow I needed to figure out how.

After doing some research I found out that the whole Savings and Loans crisis was unravelling before my eyes. The Savings and Loans crisis was the failure of 747 financial institutions that accepted savings deposits and made mortgages, car loans and other personal loans in the 1980s and 1990s. The total cost of the crisis is now estimated to be around $160.1 billion – $124.6 billion of which was directly paid by the US government through a financial bailout.

We decided we needed to get educated about this as fast as possible, because as part of the bailout the US government was practically giving real estate away for cents on the dollar. Bankers were telling me that they were receiving house keys in the mail, as thousands of Americans literally walked away from their mortgages during the Savings and Loans because their house or home unit had dropped significantly in value and they couldn't sell at a price to clear their mortgage debt. The economy was not strong, and many people couldn't make their monthly mortgage payments because they had lost their jobs.

An opportunity was happening right in front of me. I could see it, but I had no idea how to get in on it. So I bought books and 'how-to' tapes to learn how to make money in real estate. Because I didn't know anybody in Dallas, there was nobody to tell me all the reasons that the advice in those books and tapes wouldn't work – I didn't have any friends or a support system to show me the ways things 'should' be done or talk me out of what I was doing. What I was learning simply made sense, so I just followed exactly what the books and tapes said. I listened to the tapes during the day, and on the weekends and at night Jane would join me and we'd listen together.

Friends are great to talk to but terrible to listen to.

In fact, I'd already bought a dozen houses from banks before my new American friends tried to convince me that the banks didn't have anything to sell! All the Dallas locals were too scared to buy – property was being sold at ten cents on the dollar, but the locals wouldn't touch it because they would say, 'We've seen values drop 90%, what makes you think they won't drop further?'

As a new immigrant to America, I saw this as a great opportunity for me as an Australian – who was familiar and comfortable with real estate, who thought differently from the locals – to invest for a better future. Looking back now, I can see the new immigrant thinking in action.

The government was virtually giving property away at cents on the dollar, because it was in charge of the financial bailout, but the catch was that you needed cash to get in. The problem was that I didn't have a lot of cash, and it was a very difficult environment to get a bank loan in, as the banks had pulled back on their lending. For example, even if I bought a home unit for $8,000 and rented it for $667 a month, which is $8,004 a year, the bankers were too afraid to lend. They were local, and had seen the prices drop from $70,000 to $30,000 down to $8,000 and their perspective was, 'What makes you think it won't keep falling to $4,000?'

All the lenders told the same story: there was no money anywhere. But this was too good an opportunity to ignore. I had to find another way.

All the Dallas locals were too scared to buy property, but when I outlined the situation to my Aussie friends, they thought it was unbelievable because it just sounded too cheap. I needed them to come and see for themselves – then I knew they'd get excited and see the opportunity like I did.

That was around the same time that we were getting married, so I thought that I'd invite my Aussie friends over for the wedding, and I could show them the real estate while they were there.

Meanwhile, with all the bank closures, the government stopped banks from lending money for real estate. This depressed the prices even further, and it seemed that everybody was walking away from their homes and nobody was buying.

MONEY IS NEVER AN OBSTACLE

My Aussie friends came over, enjoyed the wedding, and got excited over the property opportunities – just like I knew they would. I still had no cash to get in on the deals, so I suggested to all the Aussies that for each house they invested in, they'd buy one for me. And they did. The trade-off was that while I didn't have much cash, I had local knowledge and the time to source properties, which they didn't have as they were still living in Australia. It worked because our joint venture agreement was equally balanced on both sides. We called it the 'Aussie two-for-one deal', and we bought home units, apartment buildings and houses.

Then I discovered why the locals couldn't make money out of property.

While what the locals did seemed like a perfectly normal and natural way of doing things to them, from an outsider's perspective (particularly an Australian perspective), the processes simply made no sense.

Here's what they would do as standard: at each complex of home units, they would keep two units that were not rented. They'd keep one for the manager to live in for free, and the other set up as an office for tenants to submit their maintenance requests and for the manager to collect the rent and lease units.

Be prepared to do what others won't ... make a new 'standard'.

Knowing the system we used in Australia and New Zealand, I brought in a new 'standard process' where tenants deposited their rent directly into my bank account each month and phoned in their maintenance requests to my manager who was now working from her home. When a unit became vacant, my manager would run an ad in the local paper and meet the prospective tenants at the unit for lease. It seemed to me that if tenants had someone in the office to talk to, it encouraged them to make unnecessary maintenance requests. Funnily enough, when the manager disappeared, so did most of the maintenance requests, and my revenue increased.

Most importantly, my new standard created another stream of additional income because I could now rent out the two units that previously been used for the manager and the office.

At the same time I implemented another new standard. I wanted the tenants to pay for their own electricity like we do in Australia and New Zealand – in the USA, often it's included in the rent; the owner pays for the electricity instead of the tenant. Naturally, since tenants didn't have to pay for their own electricity they didn't monitor their consumption. Dallas temperatures can vary dramatically because it's very hot in the summer (40°C) and cold in the winter (0°C), which meant my electricity bills were high. So I found a way to encourage my tenants to *want to* do things differently – we offered the tenants a $25 reduction in their rent per month, which they loved, and let them know that they were all now responsible for their own electricity, which had been costing me $75 a month per unit until then. My manager said I'd have major problems with tenants moving out because of the new charges, but that didn't happen.

By introducing these new standards we:

- decreased the number of monthly maintenance requests
- rented two additional units
- no longer paid tenants' electrical bills
- streamlined how we received rent payments.

Overall, our revenue increased substantially.

So that's how it started. I saw an opportunity where everyone else saw a problem, and I changed what needed to be changed to make it financially viable. From then on I could see that property could be a money machine that could give you more money than you put in each week. So I kept buying more property.

The more transactions I did, the more 'problems' (aka 'opportunities') I saw, and the more ways I found to do things a little differently. Without friends around to tell me all the reasons it wouldn't work, I just looked at each problem and said, 'What would happen if we did it this way?'

Overall, in our first year together, Jane and I bought 76 properties. We put some on our credit cards, we did two-for-one deals with the Aussies for others, and the US government gave us loans for some too. I was always figuring out creative ways to buy the properties, because there were no bank loans available anywhere, except from the US government.

Winners have results ... losers have excuses.

The first place that we bought and moved into was at The Plaza in Dallas, and we paid $8,000 for it. It was a two-bedroom home unit in a rapidly changing neighbourhood. This home unit had been valued at $70,000 the previous year – then it fell to $30,000, then to $20,000, then to $10,000. Finally, we bought it at auction for $8,000. Eventually, we bought about 25 properties at The Plaza.

The Plaza: Rick and Jane's first home unit

A low-market area – but we'd paid it off!

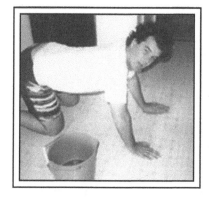

Rick scrubbing the floor of an investment unit in The Plaza – there has to be a better way!

My family thought I was crazy!

To say it was a 'low-market' area would be an understatement! None of our friends could believe we lived there, because they all lived in much nicer apartments. And Jane said to them, 'But it's free! We've already paid it off! We put it on our credit card and paid it off!' We were prepared to do things that others wouldn't consider, and Jane's girlfriends and family thought she was crazy.

We had some houses that were very expensive, too. We had a mixed bag of property. We had one property that was near multimillionaire

Ross Perot's house in Dallas, Texas. We had what we classified as A-, B- and C-grade property. We happened to live in the low-valued C-grade property, but we had others in reasonable parts of town, as well as in places that were the equivalent of Sydney's Double Bay. We could have lived in any of them, but we chose to live in our little home unit at The Plaza, because that was the place that we could afford while building our property portfolio.

CREATE PEACE OF MIND

I've noticed that a lot of people try to squeeze every cent out of a transaction. For me, that approach is too stressful. People often make such an emotional investment in the transaction, because they don't know what they really want. Once you know what you want, it's easy to let go of a little profit, and leave some profit in there for the next person. We saw the profit in the quality of life and the peace of mind that the transactions provided.

Here's the thing: we knew what we wanted, and what we didn't want. We were very clear about that. We put in the time and energy to design our life. It was all about quality of life, and we had defined exactly what that meant to us. We knew that we:

- didn't want to commute
- didn't want to be 'stuck'
- wanted to spend our time with people we cared about
- didn't want to be tied down by a job
- didn't want to be working to pay off debts

- wanted the money, time and flexibility to travel
- wanted the money, time and flexibility to support causes that were close to our hearts.

It was important for both of us to stay in touch with our family and friends in Australia and America. And it's not like those countries are right next door to each other – they're on opposite sides of the world! We wanted to be global citizens and live in either or both of our home countries, as we wished. So we knew we had to come up with a system that would let us do what we wanted.

Many people don't actually know what they want. They think they want to make money, but they don't know what they want to spend it on, or what they want to do with their time after the money has been made. When you get clear about what you really want, it's pretty simple to find the systems and processes to help you get it. **When you don't know what you really want, no system will help you get there, and no amount of money will ever fulfil you.** Houses are just widgets that let you achieve what you want. The house business and all of the systems and processes were just created to give Jane and me the quality of life we longed for – the quality of life we had already mapped out in detail.

When we first started looking at properties in America, all I knew about property was the negative gearing model I had learnt when I had owned property in Australia. I had been told that to build wealth with property you had to get yourself into a whole bunch of debt. But I was looking for another model. Houses weren't the motivator – quality of life was our motivation to build our property portfolio from scratch.

But like I said at the beginning of the chapter, this is as much Jane's story as mine, so I'm going to get Jane to tell the next bit.

JANE'S STORY

Well, Rick was lucky because he was new in town, so he didn't really have that many friends to tell him how wrong we were. But I did. I believed strongly in what we were doing, but I faced immense resistance from my friends and family, and I had to deal with that. Although we knew what we wanted, we didn't really have a clear, step-by-step plan in the beginning. But I had faith that we could do this together, that we could make this happen.

My friends and family have always been very important to me. But I just knew in my gut that this was the right way to go, so despite what my friends and family had to say, I listened to my intuition. What it came down to was that we believed in each other and we believed that we could do it. Even though we didn't quite know the details of what 'it' was yet!

Rick used to say to me that he didn't want to be another one of those 75-year-old couples that he used to see on the tour buses in Europe. We wanted to be the youngest tourists travelling, but it seemed like our properties were nudging us into the same trap as the negative gearing model.

With 76 properties, we thought we would be millionaires. We had them all rented out, but we were losing a lot of cash flow and we didn't really understand why. It took us about nine months to figure it out: expenses were eating into the rent that we received each month.

The problem was that we had 76 properties and things weren't working the way we thought they would. We had figured out how to find them and how to buy them. But keeping them was turning out to be way more expensive than we had anticipated. We'd get our statement every month, and where we should have had $20,000 every month we only had a couple of thousand. We could never quite reach the pot of gold. We said to ourselves, 'What can we do to turn this around? Because we can't live with this'. We didn't know what to do, but we knew we had to solve our problem.

We figured that we needed a way to improve our cash flow, so that we could stop getting bogged down in the administration and management expenses, which were draining us emotionally and financially.

That was when we realised that we couldn't keep all the properties, because we weren't covering all the bills. So Rick and I started to create a system that would bring our profits forward, and help other people realise their dream of home ownership at the same time.

This was a key moment for us. This was the moment that we started doing what we've done ever since, and it was when we first asked the question: 'What if we could create a better system, that gives the other person what he or she wants first, and lets us have what we want by default?'

Most people would have held onto that portfolio of properties in the hope of capturing all of the future sales when the prices climbed again. With houses and with stocks alike, most people hold out to the bitter end for the top price. They get emotionally attached to a property, and they find reasons not to sell. But this comes at a cost. Most people would rather march towards bankruptcy than give up profit, because they've invested so much emotion into the property – and instead of 'buy and hold', it becomes 'buy and hold on'. Most people wouldn't be willing to let go. But we were – we had to be. There had to be an ebb and flow, otherwise we would have been marching towards bankruptcy like everyone else. Our reasoning was that it would be better to have half of something than all of nothing. We decided that we needed to give up a percentage of our portfolio in order to keep the rest of it afloat.

So we decided to turn our tenants into buyers, and things became much simpler. We didn't have as many houses left in our portfolio, but by learning to let some of the houses go we actually had real cash flow for the first time. And although the solution was working well for us, we hadn't yet grasped exactly how powerful it could be to sell property this way.

I was actually Rick's first student – he taught me all about vendor finance. Rick loves putting the transactions together, that's always been his passion. But when we realised we needed to sell properties as well, that became my job.

It was scary to begin with – I had no experience with sales, I wasn't good with numbers, we didn't have a manual for seller (or vendor) finance, there was no live training and nothing was written down. Everything we needed to know was all in Rick's head. I knew I had to find buyers for the houses as quickly and painlessly as possible and to begin with, Rick helped me write the ads to put in the newspaper. Then the phone started ringing. Rick taught me to pre-screen and pre-qualify potential buyers. In the beginning my phone conversations tended to be quite long, but with his help I managed to reduce the time per call to just a few minutes. One of the golden rules I learnt was not to project my personal beliefs onto my buyers. Once I stopped saying to myself, 'I would never live in that property – why would anyone else want to live there?' things started to fall into place. I also learnt that I needed to know that my buyers loved the house AND they could afford it.

I also struggled with the image of what a 'salesperson' was, and I couldn't see myself selling anything to anyone. But I could see myself talking to people. I had no formal sales training, but I knew I could talk to people. With Rick's help I soon discovered that I could make genuine connections with people, talk naturally with them from the heart, and help them realise their dream of home ownership. When I saw it that way, I realised that I could just be me, and I began to really enjoy helping people buy their homes from us.

What we hadn't anticipated was how fulfilling it would be to give people the chance to be owners instead of tenants. We realised that we weren't just doing a transaction, we were helping people realise the dream of home ownership – which, for some of them, had been seemingly impossible. We soon discovered how rewarding that was, and how good it felt every single time we completed a transaction. What I've always loved about seller finance is that it only works if everyone wins, because both the buyer and the seller are agreeing about what's possible.

I found a sense of purpose by solving people's problems and, over time, our students have found the same thing. Most of them say they got started for the money, but that the money becomes secondary. They keep doing it because it feels good to help people.

How vendor finance works

N ow is the best time ever to be getting into property. We live in a world that has gone through recent turmoil in the financial markets, and bank loans are more and more difficult to get, yet people still have the desire to buy and sell their houses. If you can be willing to look at things a little differently, and try out some new ideas, this could be the most profitable time of your life!

There are two parts to every property. You may have heard them called other names, but I like to call them the 'cash bit' and the 'debt bit', because everyone can understand that.

Equity = Asset = Cash Bit
Mortgage = Liability = Debt Bit

I'm in the business of solving property problems. In general, property problems fall into two categories – the need to sell a house quickly to either get access to the cash bit or to remove the pain of the debt bit, or the need to either qualify for a bank loan or save up a deposit to be able to realise the dream of home ownership. Historically, whenever bank loans have been difficult to get, buyers and sellers have talked directly to each other with no bank middleman. In fact, people have been using seller finance (also known as vendor finance) to support their property sales for hundreds of years.

Throughout history there have been a few major turning points that relate directly to these problems. These were events in history that completely changed the game of buying and selling houses. And when you are aware of these historical moments and their implications, you'll really understand why now is the best time ever for you to be getting into property.

When most people say, 'Vendor finance? I've never heard of it', I reply with, 'That's because you weren't buying houses in the 1950s!' When I first started talking to solicitors about this concept, the young ones didn't know anything about it, but the older, grey-haired, almost-retired property solicitors all remembered it well, because they used to do it all the time before the mid-1960s.

Originally, banks only loaned money to buy houses, not land. Land was bought using vendor finance. Then, when you owned the land, the bank would give you a loan to build your house. When banks started lending money to buy land as well as houses, vendor finance wasn't needed anymore, so it faded away into the background. But the old solicitors still remember the good old days when vendor finance was as common as sliced bread.

Nowadays, with the recent financial crisis, there has been a massive rise in mortgagee sales and a massive squeeze on bank loans. Bank loans are harder to get now than ever before. In other countries, where bank loans have always been difficult to get, vendor finance never went out of fashion. It's only because bank loans were so easy to get for a few decades that an entire generation of Australians forgot about vendor finance. But it never disappeared completely. Vendor finance has been used by some people, and in some towns, all the way through. *Now* you understand why right now is the perfect time for vendor finance to make a big comeback. The problems we're all facing in today's market conditions are the exact problems that vendor finance strategies solve.

I've invited Anthony Cordato, from Cordato Partners Lawyers, to tell you about the history of vendor finance in this country. Tony bought and sold his own properties using vendor finance in the 1970s, 1980s and 1990s, and as a business and property solicitor he has processed the paperwork for almost 2,500 vendor finance transactions for his clients in the last ten years. He's not called 'Australia's Vendor Finance Lawyer' for nothing!

INTERVIEW WITH TONY CORDATO – PROPERTY AND BUSINESS SOLICITOR

What's your experience with vendor finance?

As a property solicitor I've processed the paperwork for almost 2,500 vendor finance property transactions over the past decade. I originally started my career working in a subdivision firm, subdividing estates up and down the east coast of Australia. I learnt that when you're selling blocks of land, you get less money if you sell for cash, because there are fewer buyers around who can afford to pay in cash. Most purchasers needed finance to buy the land. Without finance it was not possible; with finance there were more buyers to sell to – and finance allowed us to sell for more money. All we were doing in the 1970s and 1980s was offering vendor terms to sell land, same as they were doing in 1870s and 1880s.

What is vendor finance?

Vendor finance is also known as 'seller finance', 'terms contracts' or 'vendor terms'. It means that the seller of a property (the vendor) offers easy payment terms. So the buyer, instead of paying the full amount up-front, can pay the property off in a number of instalments over time.

'Vendor terms' contracts are just the same as finance from a finance company, where the purchaser pays instalments over time. Very few people have enough cash to buy property because it's such a big purchase, so they get finance from a bank, credit union, or finance company. With vendor finance, the seller says, 'I will be the bank, just make your payments to me instead'.

There are different types of paperwork to support a vendor finance transaction, but the paperwork is only part of the equation. But before you worry about the paperwork, you need to know how you can structure the transaction so it works for the buyer and the seller. It's the structure that makes the transaction work, not just the vendor finance paperwork!

What does 'structure' mean?

As the seller, you need to structure the vendor finance terms according to the buyer's situation. Broadly speaking, there are three situations: if the buyer wants to buy today, but they don't have a bank loan, then you use an instalment contract (see chapter 15); if they can get a bank loan, but they're short on a deposit, you'll offer them deposit finance (see chapter 16); if the buyer is interested in buying in future, then you use a rent-to-own (see chapter 18).

It's also important to know exactly how much to ask for, how much you want up-front, what the ongoing payments will be, and how long to give them to pay it out.

There are all kinds of theoretical models. If you want to sell a property on vendor terms, it raises a lot of questions that need to be answered. Do you want to ask for $250 a week over one year? Should you charge interest? How much up-front money (deposit) should you ask for? Why would you ask for different amounts? How would you have this conversation? These are all structuring questions and they are what Rick helps his students to master.

Over the last ten years I've helped to put legal frameworks around the concepts and create new legal paperwork that is understood by other solicitors – this paperwork has become the new 'standard' for vendor finance.

What have been the major turning points for vendor finance in Australia?

I suspect vendor finance has been used in Australia since settlement in 1788. The banking system in Australia only really developed in the 1850s when the banks had some gold, courtesy of the gold rush. Prior to that finance was only accessible to merchants, not everyday people. The banking system wasn't able to cope with the great expansion in the Australian economy that followed the gold rush in the 1870s and 1880s. But people making money wanted to buy property, so the owners would offer the property on payment terms. Standard instalment terms for a house block of land in the 1880s involved paying the purchase price over four payments: 25% up-front, 25% after six months, 25% after 12 months, and the final 25% after 18 months. The purchaser had to pay 6% per annum interest on the outstanding amount. That way, the vendor could get the price they wanted – for example, the vendor was able to get £12 per block of land, instead of only the £3 the buyer might have had in his pocket at the time. And buyers were able to purchase the land immediately instead of waiting and losing the opportunity, as they were able to pay the purchase price off over time out of their earnings.

That system continued working well up until the 1960s. People would first buy the house block on vendor terms and once they had paid off the land, the bank would then provide finance to build their house. This was the 'Great Australian Dream' at its best.

Vendor finance shrank from the mid-1960s because the banks made home-loan finance more available. Prior to that time, banks gave loans for houses, but not for land. In the mid-1960s banks began to offer loans on land and home packages for the first time.

Turning points have always been dependent on how much money the banking system is willing to provide in home loans. The money ebbs and flows – there are periods when home-loan finance surges, and periods when it pulls back. From the mid-

1960s to 1974 the big finance-company offshoots of the major banks funded a surge in home loans and loans for investment properties. Then the money dried up in 1974 due to a number of factors: the Vietnam War, a high 15% inflation rate, the price of gold increasing from $35 to $200 in the early 1970s, and the oil price skyrocketing because of the world's first oil crisis. This all sparked a credit crisis, because all the money previously used for consumer credit was redirected elsewhere – it was a worldwide phenomenon.

Consumer credit recovered and settled down by the 1980s. There was another period of worldwide economic expansion, where credit was easy to get, and there was a huge commercial and residential construction boom in Australia. Inflation kept rising until it reached 7%, and interest rates hit 17% in the 1989 global credit crunch. That's when vendor finance became very popular in its current form in the USA – if someone wanted to sell their property in America during that time, they HAD to offer vendor terms because there were no residential loans available any other way. Then the mid-1990s brought the concept of securitised lending, and that easy finance drove another surge of home-loan finance lending.

Vendor finance was booming between 2000 and 2005. Then it slackened off a bit when the banks were throwing money at everyone and everything, until that all ended with the global financial crisis of 2008-2009. This easy money in the mid-2000s fuelled a huge boom in residential property. Now that the finance tap has been turned halfway off again, vendor finance has started picking up again. It's a really predictable cycle.

What does that really mean to everyday Australians?

The banks pick and choose people to lend to, and they pick and choose locations. In the current market, unless you've got a 10-20% deposit, you're not going to be able to buy a house. Because of this, many of people feel shut out of the housing market, but they don't like renting and they know they can do better. Vendor finance provides the pathway for a lot of hardworking Australians to buy their first home when the banks tighten up.

Also, most banks won't lend on properties in towns that have a population of less than 10,000 people, and that includes many smaller country towns. If you want to sell a property in those smaller towns you're likely to have to do it with vendor terms because the banks often don't fancy lending there.

What's going on right now?

Today, the banks are lending 90-92% of all residential loans. Five years ago, the banks were lending 78% of the loans, 14% of loans were being provided by securitised lenders like Aussie, Wizard, Liberty and Bluestone, and the remaining 8% were provided by credit unions. In recent years that middle 14% that the securitised (low-doc) lenders were providing has shrivelled to almost nothing, leaving a gap for anyone with vendor finance.

The banks are also tightening up their lending requirements. They have scaled back to only lending 80% of the value of the property, except to 'gold-plated' customers. Low-doc lenders are providing as little as 65% of the property value to the self-employed and credit impaired. This makes it very tough for people with less than two years of proven salary income (including self-employed people, or those new to the country). They still might be good people who can afford the payments, it's just that traditional banks won't lend them very much at the moment.

What do you foresee for the future?

I believe vendor finance has its place in the marketplace. Vendor finance provides the bridge between where someone starts off, and where they want to be with their long-term housing loan via the banking system. The objective is to prove yourself to be a good payer on vendor finance, so you'll be able to refinance through the banking system in two to three years. The banking system will always offer better rates, and while vendor finance won't replace traditional finance sources, it is a very useful part of the system and can be an important stepping stone for homebuyers.

Some people tell me that vendor finance is illegal, but the governments won't abolish vendor finance, because they use it themselves. An example of this is the large housing estates in the Mount Druitt area in western Sydney from 1968 to 1978. Instead of renting, the government sold these housing estates to lower-income earners on 40-year instalment contracts. Governments are still selling on vendor terms in NSW and other states as well.

The National Consumer Credit Code (*National Consumer Credit Protection Act, 2009*) applies to instalment contracts, and recognises them as fully legitimate forms of consumer credit. It is all covered by current legislation. People tell me instalment contracts are illegal, but that's just because they don't know about the Credit Code. The government says it's all completely legal. A terms contract wording can be found on the standard contract of sale in Western Australia and Victoria. So if you're using vendor terms in those states you just have to tick the box.

As we know, interest rates have gone up and down over the years, and bank loans have been easier to get at some times, and harder to get at others. Vendor finance has been used in the background to sell property all this time, and has been gaining more and more popularity in recent years. Since more people have been using vendor finance, especially the rent-to-own lease-option strategy, the federal government even included the following question on the 2011 census, asking if people were purchasing their home under a rent/buy scheme:

56 Is this dwelling:

- Including owners of caravans, manufactured homes or houseboats regardless of whether or not the site is owned.
- Remember to mark box like this: ▬

( ) Owned outright? ▶ **Go to 59**
( ) Owned with a mortgage? ▶ **Go to 58**
( ) Being purchased under a rent/buy scheme?
( ) Being rented?
( ) Being occupied rent free?
( ) Being occupied under a life tenure scheme
( ) Other?

Summary

Vendor finance is as important a part of the finance system as credit unions. I see the banks settling at about 80% of the loans, credit unions providing 10%, and vendor finance filling the remaining 10%. If the banking system is not healthy, vendor finance will expand to fill the available gap in the market. The paperwork system is available. All that's needed is for more people to know how to use it properly!

6

Solving the unsolvable

You can't solve today's new problems with yesterday's old processes.

– Rick Otton

Many people come to my students and me with problems that seem unsolvable. And it's true – their problems can't be solved using traditional systems and processes. But they can be solved. What they don't realise is that it's *always* possible to create a solution – all you need to do is look at the situation a little differently.

Here are the two most common 'unsolvable' problems we see:

- **Negative gearing** → how to turn a negatively geared property around and make it cash flow positive instead.

- **Upside down loan** → how to sell a property when the loan exceeds the market price, so you don't wind up going to the settlement table with a big cheque to cover the balance.

These problems may actually apply to the same property – it will usually be a property that costs too much to hold onto, and is sucking so much money out of the owner's pocket that they think they can't afford to keep it anymore.

So, those are the problems – here's how we solve them.

The only decision the owner needs to make is whether they want to sell the property or keep it. Either way, we can turn it around and make it profitable for them.

If they want to continue to own the property we can do a **negative gearing turnaround**, and rent it out to a future homeowner. If they want to sell it, we can create an **upside down loan** and sell it on vendor terms. Here's how it works:

NEGATIVE GEARING TURNAROUND

People often buy property with the intention of holding it long term and realising the capital growth in the future. But the holding costs can be extreme, especially if the rental income on an investment property doesn't cover the costs of ownership.

In a negative gearing turnaround, you rent the property to a future homeowner instead of renting the property to a tenant in the normal way. It's more of a shift in thinking – the tenant will make rental payments as though they were making mortgage payments. This is great for tenants who either don't have a deposit, or have something preventing them from getting a traditional bank loan. They have the emotional buy-in of home ownership, and you just charge them the same rates as a bank loan.

When you turn tenants into buyers their payments are higher each month than regular monthly rental rates, which transforms your negatively geared property into a cash flow positive one.

For example, a house worth $400,000 would usually bring in $400 a week in rental income, which wouldn't cover the costs of holding it. If you have a 30-year loan on the property ($400,000 at 7% pa principal and interest), all you need to do is calculate the charges for your tenant/ buyer on a 25-year loan instead of a 30-year one, and the difference generates *positive* monthly cash flow for you.

HOLDING COSTS	RENTAL INCOME	TENANT/BUYER
30-year mortgage		*25-year mortgage*
$2,661 per month	$1,733 per month	$2,827 per month
$614 per week	$400 per week	$652 per week
	$214 per week shortfall	$38 per week profit

The tenant will either move out or refinance and buy the property in two to five years. You can also do things to encourage them to stay longer or refinance sooner, depending on your preferences.

UPSIDE DOWN LOAN

Many people get caught out buying apartments 'off the plan', and what often happens is that the market value drops below the total outstanding loan after a few years. If this happens, adding value to make your property stand out as being 'easy to buy' is the solution.

A seller in this situation called me for advice. He had paid $495,000 for a high-rise home unit, for which he had obtained 100% finance by using his home as security. But now, the property was only worth around $455,000, and if he sold at that price he'd need to bring $40,000 cash to the settlement to pay out the loss.

His loan was $495,000 × 7% over 30 years = $3,293.25 per month.

I suggested that rather than write a cheque for $40,000 (which he did not have), he should simply market the property for $495,000 and provide a loan to a new buyer who could give him a $20,000 deposit up-front. The seller would carry back the balance of $475,000 over 25 years at 9.5% per annum (which was the same as the interest rate on low-doc loans at the time).

Most buyers would need $100,000 for a 20% deposit for a regular bank loan, so reducing the deposit to $20,000 made his apartment much easier for people to buy.

This meant that the new buyer could purchase the property with just $20,000 deposit, and repayments of $4,150.06 a month – and best of all, the new buyer wouldn't need to qualify for a bank loan. Even though there was more than one unit listed for sale in the seller's building, this approach made his property easier to buy than all the rest of the units for sale.

Think about your local convenience store – it sells bread, milk and butter, sometimes at double the price you'd pay elsewhere. But you still buy bread, milk and butter there, because it's not about the price; it's about the convenience. And a house can be exactly the same – you want to make sure that yours is a more convenient option for new buyers.

If the buyer continued to pay the seller the full monthly payment of $4,150.06, it would pay the original loan out in full in just 17 years, earning the seller $4,150.06 per month of positive cash flow income for the remaining eight years of the original term. A lockout clause in the paperwork would prevent the new purchaser from refinancing too early, before the loan amount payable to the bank is less than the amount payable by the buyers; and an equitable title clause allows the new buyer to resell the property themselves while the vendor's loan is still in place. This is a far cry from having to pay out $40,000 at settlement by doing things the traditional way!

A house that is easy to buy is easy to sell. The reason this works is because you are making it available to 100% of the marketplace, instead of it only being available to the percentage of people who have a $100,000 deposit and can qualify for a bank loan.

7

A different way of thinking

Whenever you find yourself on the side of the majority, it is time to pause and reflect.

– Mark Twain

One day a friend and I were discussing cultural differences between Aussies and Kiwis. My friend is from New Zealand and I'm from Australia, and he first told me about **the convict and the warrior.**

As you know, many of our forefathers were originally shipped from England to Australia as convicts on the First Fleet. When they arrived, they were numbered and stripped of any individual identity. When one of the convicts spoke up, they were not punished as an individual. Instead all the convicts would be punished as a group. It is thought that the expression, 'Stop being a tall poppy' dates back to those days, and this has been handed down from one generation to the next. It was used in the context of, 'Stop being a tall poppy because otherwise the rest of us will get punished'.

When I started investigating tall poppy syndrome, I discovered that there is an ongoing debate about whether it's an Australian characteristic or a national myth.

The Macquarie Dictionary defines tall poppy syndrome as, ' ... *a desire to diminish in stature those people who have attained excellence'*. The Australian National Dictionary says a tall poppy is, '*a person who is conspicuously successful; frequently one whose distinction, rank or wealth attracts envious notice or hostility'*.

I believe it's still alive and well today; in fact, it seems to be a permanent fixture in Australian culture – more so than in New Zealand culture. My theory is that the tall poppy syndrome is born from our convict beginnings, implying that as Aussies, we are more comfortable with under-achievement.

People who immigrated to New Zealand had to pay their own way with no guarantee of their future. They came as 'free' settlers, not as convicts. New Zealanders are a warrior nation. My belief is that they had to achieve to survive and consequently they had to be tall poppies and become more entrepreneurial. They had to develop the determination to see it through and make it work.

New Zealanders and Americans are similar in that they appreciate successful people, emulating and admiring them, while we Australians sometimes resent the success of our fellow peers.

When I lived in the United States I discovered that every child is taught that he or she can grow up to be president – they are raised with the belief that, 'If you can dream it, you can be it'. Wow! What a contrast from how I grew up with tall poppy syndrome in Australia.

I realised then that the way we think is handed down by the people before us. This has an enormous influence on our ability to move forward, because any kind of backward thinking makes moving forward difficult. That's why some people get bad results in boom times, and some people get great results in bad times. It's got little to do with 'good times' or 'bad times' – it all comes down to how you think, how you see things, and what you do.

Over the years I've figured out that 95% of people don't go anywhere. The 5% who do get somewhere think differently. So I've always found that the simplest thing is to just look at what the majority of people are doing, and then do the opposite. On average you're bound to come out ahead!

Here's something I find fascinating, and it really puts this 'different thinking' idea into perspective:

The majority of self-made millionaires in any country are new immigrants.

Why is that? If we can figure that out, maybe we can think like a new immigrant and get similar results.

New immigrants often can't go back to their old country, so their backs are really against the wall and they have to deliver results to survive. They have ideas, perspectives and habits from their old country, not their new one, so they automatically think differently to everyone else around them. They often don't have a group of 'that'll never work' friends influencing them or holding them back or trying to get them to *stop* thinking differently. They don't have anyone to lose face in front of. And they didn't grow up being told the same version of 'that's just the way things are' like all the people around them.

As a result, they ask obvious or awkward questions that others don't, and they challenge otherwise-unquestioned processes and accepted conventions. They find a better, more efficient way. They think differently and do things differently. They've got nothing to lose: not money, friends, reputation, status ... nothing. And usually, they have themselves and their family to take care of, and with no fallback plans, they have to make it or die trying. New immigrants have *everything* to gain.

'That's great, Rick, but I'm not a new immigrant,' I hear you say. Well here's one thing I know is true:

It's never too late to *think* like a new immigrant.

You see, it's not actually *being* a new immigrant that makes the difference. It's *thinking* like a new immigrant that makes the difference. And anyone can do that. Anyone. Anytime.

I did. And it was thinking like a new immigrant that got me started in property in the first place.

JUST SUPPOSE THERE WAS ANOTHER WAY ...

I'm always looking for better ways to do things. So I'm always asking, 'Why can't I do it this way?' And when we investigate why, we often find it's simply because it hasn't been done that way before, or it hasn't been done that way for a long time. But apart from that, if there's no legal, moral or ethical reason why something can't be done, why not do it that way? We can create a new way.

We all have a system in our heads of how we think things have to be, and how we think things have to be done. This is known as 'process'. And if something can't be done using the process we have in our heads, we usually just think it can't be done at all. But that's simply not true. It may not be possible *that* way, but there is *another* way. And if we don't know a way that works already, we just have to figure out what it is.

If you just start to ask this one question, it'll change your results and your life forever:

'Is this the best way, or simply the hand-me-down way that no one has ever changed?'

> *Every truth passes through three stages before it is recognised. In the first it is ridiculed, in the second it is violently opposed, in the third it is regarded as self-evident.*
>
> – Arthur Schopenhauer

When I figure out a new way of doing things, I don't look at the surface. I look at the process, and at how we can change things in the process to make it possible to solve real problems. **And from this perspective I create systems, methods and processes that benefit the other person first.**

I do this because:

1. people don't really want what they first say they want, and
2. when you help people get what they *really* want, you automatically get what *you* want.

So, how do we change?

The only time most people move forward in life is when their back is up against the wall and there's no way out (and they start thinking differently, like a new immigrant). They wake up one day and figure out that where they are is nowhere near where they want to be.

If someone says, 'It'll never work,' is that based on the process that they know, or is it based on the process I'm about to create? You see, there's no such thing as, 'We can't do that'. We can do anything. There are just some things we haven't figured out a process for yet.

I don't know about you, but whenever there's a new challenge or opportunity that needs a new process, I'm excited to figure out how to do it.

THE RULE OF THREE

Whenever you hear, 'We can't do that', or, 'We don't do it that way' from a big organisation ... call them back! That's right - call them back. I call it The Rule of Three.

It's very hard to get two people to agree on anything - especially which rules to follow - and every time you call, someone different usually answers the phone. For example, if you're trying to get a new phone line installed:

- Call once and they'll be able to do it in three weeks.
- Call back and you're down to three days.
- Call a third time and it'll be done this afternoon.

Whenever you're told that something can't be done, just keep calling back until you get the answer you want!

HOW DO WE START TO THINK THAT WAY?

How do we start thinking the way we do in the first place? Because once we know how we started thinking that way, we'll know how to start thinking in a new way if we want to. Like thinking like a new immigrant perhaps.

A man will be imprisoned in a room with a door that's unlocked and opens inwards; as long as it does not occur to him to pull rather than push.

– Ludwig Wittgenstein

I learnt that the way we think about things is stored in different parts of our brain. Some things are stored in the front, and other things are stored in the back. Scientists call the front bit the frontal lobe, and the back bit the amygdala, but I find it easier to remember if I call them the 'front bit' and the 'back bit'.

There has been a lot of research done on this lately. It's very interesting, but the main reason we've been lucky enough to find out about this is because there has been a massive increase in depression in recent years and the government has sponsored research to try to understand this growing problem. The research discovered that depression is stored in the back bit. And it just so happens that life history, process and scripts are stored in the back bit, too.

So, every time you hear about something new or have a new idea (front bit) and you get motivated to do something about it (front bit), that new idea and motivation have a committee meeting with the back bit to see if they can all agree before taking any sort of consistent action.

FRONTAL LOBE
• Inclination
• New ideas
• Motivation
• Passion

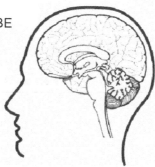

AMYGDALA
• Life history
• Process
• Scripts
• Worry
• Self-doubt
• Stress
• Depression

If you think that there's a way, even if you have no idea how yet, somehow you'll find a way.

Now if your life history (back bit), patterns of worry or self-doubt (back bit), and your ingrained process (back bit) don't match with the new idea (front bit), the back bit of the committee is going to win and you'll keep doing the same thing you've always been doing.

Try this. Cross your arms. Now uncross them and cross them with the other arm on top. Or try brushing your teeth with the hand you don't usually use. That awkward, unfamiliar feeling you get is what it feels like when you oppose a process that has been developed and reinforced in the back bit of your brain over many years.

This explains why it's infinitely easier for a child to learn a foreign language before the age of seven. Language is a combination of life history, process and scripts. If a child learns two languages at the same time before the critical age, neither language has to fight with the other to get access to the back bit of the brain. They both go straight in.

Entrepreneurs challenge accepted processes and make things more efficient than they used to be. They're up against the establishment, the traditionalists and the standard. Entrepreneurs recognise the opportunity for change, they tackle the process, make it more efficient, and before long, it becomes the new standard. I believe that, with training, it is possible to think like an entrepreneur at any age.

> *He is able who thinks he is able.*
> – Buddha

House prices seem so far out of reach for so many people when you look at it the traditional way. This often leaves people feeling helpless, weak and defeated. And when they feel that way, they just give up. But it doesn't have to be that way – you just need to think about it differently.

I'm leading a movement of like-minded people who want to seize the opportunity for home ownership in a new way. I'm here to empower people to transform the way they buy and sell properties, so that they can actually start to get what they want.

Remember, in any transaction, the deal should come first. You can always find a paperwork system, or create one, to support the transaction. And the deal can be whatever two people want to do and can agree on. Over the last 20 years Jane and I have changed the processes, so the systems are already there, ready and waiting for you to use whenever you decide to use them. I believe that 90% of creating a successful transaction is how you think about it. That's the biggest step of all.

There's always a way

People often ask me, 'How do you think that way?' Well, now you know. And now you can think that way too. You can do anything you want – it may take some time to figure out how, but you can *always* find a way.

I have seen so many different ways of doing things in the property market that I *know* that no matter what problem you're trying to solve, there is always a way. And by the time you've read through the next few chapters, you'll have enough references of your own that you'll know there's always a way, too.

Even with all my experience, sometimes I'm stumped. But whenever I hear that little voice in the back of my head say, 'You can't do that,' I don't dismiss it. I deal with it the same way I deal with anyone else saying, 'You can't do that' to me. I acknowledge it, and I realise that what it's really saying is that you can't do that *based on the old familiar process*. But that was then ... this is NOW!

And so I say, 'Of course you can't do it based on the *old* process. But you can do

**That was then.
This is now!**

it with the *new* process'. And then I get busy using, finding or creating a new process that we *can* use to do what I want to do.

Everything you don't know yet is simply an undiscovered process

I was fortunate that I could bring in Australian processes that I was familiar and comfortable with, and apply them to USA property problems in a way that seemed new. I've also been fortunate enough to have been exposed to some of the different processes that are standard in the USA and around the world, and I've brought them back here to Australia and New Zealand to share them with you.

Total freedom: time, money, travel, fun ...

I n the house business, you're basically in the business of making nightmares go away and making dreams come true. People only buy and sell houses to avoid a pain or make a gain. So, either you're solving problems and making their pain go away, or you're helping them access cash to make their dreams come true. Which means that it's *essential* to know what your – and the buyer or seller's – most important 'pains and gains' really are.

Success in the house business comes down to three simple things:

- knowing what's really important to you
- knowing what's really important to your buyer or seller
- putting processes and paperwork systems in place to support you both getting what you really, really want.

If you can do that, you can do anything. All my most successful students have this in common. They know what they really want and why it's so important to them. They sidestep the superficial, throwaway reasons that most people give them to quickly help their buyers and sellers connect with what's really important to them. And they put paperwork systems in place that give everyone what they really want.

So let's take a look at what's really important to you.

If you think you're doing this for the money, you're wrong. Nobody does anything for the money. They do it for what they believe the money will give them and how that will make them feel. Let me repeat that:

They do it for what they believe the money will give them and how that will make them feel.

And that's different for everybody. You need to know the real reason why you're doing what you're doing. You also need to know where you're starting from, what resources you have access to, and what might be possible if you choose to do it. But of all these things, the WHY is the most important. A strong enough reason WHY will carry you through while the HOW works itself out.

> *The essence of knowledge is, having it, to apply it; not having it, to confess your ignorance.*
> – Confucius

So many people think that they could do anything, if only they knew HOW. They think that not knowing how is what's preventing them from doing what they want to do. But that's simply not true. Have you ever learnt how to do something and then not done it? I know I have. Hundreds of times. I've learnt how to go to the gym, but I don't do it as often as I know I should. I've learnt how to wash the dishes by hand, but I don't do it. Why would I, when the dishwasher is right there? I've learnt how to ride a pushbike, but if I want to go anywhere I usually drive my car instead.

WHY to do something is always more important and more valuable than HOW to do it. Most of this book is about HOW ... but only the WHY will get you to take action on what you learn. The HOW is readily available when you really decide something is important enough to do. But it only becomes important enough to do when you have a strong enough reason WHY. Without that, the HOW is irrelevant.

When you go through the process of discovering and connecting with your own personal WHY, it will make it easy and natural for you to help other people connect with theirs. Which is exactly what you will be doing when you talk to buyers and sellers. The WHY is important. The WHY is everything. The HOW is just processes and paperwork to make the WHY happen.

So, here are the big questions:

WHY do you want to buy and sell houses without a bank?

WHY is that important to you?

If you can answer these questions, then the rest will be easy.

For Jane and me, the reason WHY was clear. Sure, we knew we had to make money somehow, but we weren't doing it for the money. We were doing it because:

- we wanted to be together

- we wanted to be free to travel

- we wanted to stay close with our friends and families in both our home countries, which were on opposite sides of the planet
- we didn't want to be tied down
- we didn't want to commute
- we wanted the creative freedom to play with ideas, build things together and help people somehow.

So whatever vehicle we used to give us our financial freedom, also had to give us time freedom (so we could travel whenever we wanted to) and location freedom (so our income would keep coming in no matter which country we were in).

Answering the WHY question is simple and quick for some people, but not so quick and **easy** for others. Sometimes you have to dig a little deeper for a stronger answer that you really connect with.

Jane and I were designing our future together, and the house business helped us to do that. Some of our students wanted to get out of an unpleasant work situation, or spend more time with their families, and the house business helped them to do that. Some students with children didn't want to be working all the time, and only see their kids when they were sleeping. One couple wanted to take family holidays any time they wanted to, without having to get leave approval from work. One guy wanted to drop his kids off and pick them up from school every day.

Some students had specific property problems that they wanted to solve – for themselves or for a loved one. So they learnt how to sell a house fast and avoid foreclosure. Or they learnt how to buy a house without saving up a traditional large deposit. Or they learnt how to sell a house and make a profit when the loan is bigger than the value of the house. They learnt how to solve one specific problem, and enjoyed it so much that they kept going, solving similar problems for other people.

What kind of freedom do you choose?

The common thread running through most people's WHY is freedom. We all want some kind of freedom. And often we believe that money will give us this freedom. But freedom has a unique and specific meaning for each of us. Jane and I were designing our life together, and we got very clear about what freedom really meant to us. And our students needed to do the same thing – they had to get clear about what freedom meant to them, whether it was:

- freedom to travel

- freedom to be with loved ones

- freedom to pick the kids up from school

- freedom from mortgage stress

- freedom to own their own home

- freedom to help their favourite charity

- freedom to be creative

- freedom to help people

- freedom to work their own hours

- freedom from traffic, or

- freedom to be, do, have or create whatever was important to them.

So the next question is this: what does freedom mean to you?

There are different aspects to freedom, and some may be more or less important to you. But they all factor into your big, compelling WHY.

Financial Freedom *Flexibility to do or buy* ***whatever*** *you want* Money, income, assets, cash flow. Not having to worry about money or bills. Having homes, cars, exotic holidays. Freedom to afford school fees.	**Time Freedom** *Flexibility to do things* ***whenever*** *you want* Work your own hours. Take vacations when you want to. Spend time with friends and family, often!
Location Freedom *Flexibility to live or travel* ***wherever*** *you want* Freedom to travel whenever you want. Work from anywhere in the world, as long as you have access to a phone and email.	**Creative Freedom** *Flexibility to be inspired* *and **make a difference*** Freedom to use your gifts and talents to create, invent and make a difference. Freedom to enjoy art, film, music, learning, creativity and inspiration.

Freedom comes down to the flexibility to choose. We all make choices every day. When it feels like we have no choice, or only limited choices, we feel like we have less freedom. More freedom means more choices. So, if you had the flexibility to do whatever you want, whenever you want, wherever you want in the world, with whomever you want, and the flexibility to be inspired and make a difference, how would that make you feel?

We don't often get asked to design our lives, or to define what freedom really means to us. Maybe things would turn out differently if we did. If you take a moment to focus on what's important to you, and what freedom really means to you, that moment might help you make slightly different choices, which might lead to other slightly different choices. And pretty soon all those choices will add up to a new way of life.

I'll show you a few examples of how people have answered the questions, 'WHY do you want to buy and sell houses without a bank? WHY is that important to you?' Then you can answer them for yourself.

RICK and JANE

Financial Freedom	Time Freedom
Flexibility to do or buy **whatever** *you want*	*Flexibility to do things* **whenever** *you want*
Plenty of uninterrupted income to enable us to do whatever we want, have heaps of fun, and travel the world while we're still young enough to enjoy it!	Not working for a boss. Not being tied to traditional nine-to-five hours. Travel whenever we feel like it.
Location Freedom	**Creative Freedom**
Flexibility to live or travel **wherever** *you want*	*Flexibility to be inspired* *and* **make a difference**
Have homes in the USA and Australia and visit both countries often. Keep running our business no matter where we are in the world. Have our income keep flowing in while we're travelling.	To be creative and build something great together. Even though we're not sure what we want to build, we know we want to build something, and we want to do it together.

JADE (single mum)

Financial Freedom	Time Freedom
Flexibility to do or buy **whatever** *you want*	*Flexibility to do things* **whenever** *you want*
To replace my corporate IT income, without the stress or the work hours. Good home, good suburb and private school fees. Go back to uni and still have my income coming in while I study and travel.	Spend as much fun time as possible with my kids and my family. Have time to play after school every day. Take proper care of my health with retreats, great food, massages, rest, surfing and yoga.
Location Freedom	Creative Freedom
Flexibility to live or travel **wherever** *you want*	*Flexibility to be inspired* *and* **make a difference**
Work from home, be at home after school. Be able to travel when and where I want to. Be able to take my kids to experience different things around the world.	Read a lot, sing a lot and learn a lot! Hang out with cool, inspiring, creative people. Help people who make a real difference to reach more people and impact more lives.

Now, answer the same questions for yourself:

WHY do you want to buy and sell houses without a bank?

WHY is that important to you?

Financial Freedom *Flexibility to do or buy* ***whatever** you want*	**Time Freedom** *Flexibility to do things* ***whenever** you want*
Location Freedom *Flexibility to live or travel* ***wherever** you want*	**Creative Freedom** *Flexibility to be inspired* *and **make a difference***

THERE IS NO SUCH THING AS A BETTER WAY, JUST THE BEST WAY FOR YOU. IT ALL WORKS!

There comes a time when you have to stop learning, roll up your sleeves and start taking action. My main objective is not that you learn a bunch of cool trivia that you mention once in a while at dinner parties. My main objective is that you use the things you learn in this book to start to living life on your own terms. That's why it's important for you to get a little clearer on what 'living life on your own terms' looks and feels like to you.

Clarity is powerful. Only when you know where you are and where you're going can you choose which steps to take. Now you know WHY this is so important to you, let's take a closer look at HOW you'll get there.

ALL ABOUT BUYING

We all buy property for different reasons. Some people buy their own home for a sense of security and peace of mind. Some people just want to stop paying dead rent. And some people buy property as an investment that will grow in value over time.

Maybe you've tried to buy a property at a discount in the past and it hasn't worked. Maybe you found the home of your dreams, but had it slip through your fingers because the deposit required was just too high. Maybe you bought a property, but it cost too much to hold onto, so you had to sell it before you could realise any real capital growth. Many people have been in the same situations.

No matter why you're interested in buying property, chances are you'd love to:

- buy at a discount
- pay as little money up-front as possible
- be able to hold onto the property while it grows in value.

Most people have trouble achieving even one of these goals. But by the end of the next few chapters, you'll know how to do all three – in any market.

Discounts and creative structuring of deals are everywhere, but they are not always where you think you'll find them. The strategies I'm about to show you will help you discover how to find great opportunities – you just need to look at things a little differently, and think creatively, so you can find a way for the buyer and seller to **both** get what they really want.

It is very important to define what type of property you're buying, and be crystal clear about what you want, before you start looking. Ask yourself these questions:

Is this property going to be your home? Or is this property an investment?

Here's why it's important you have clarity on how you answer these questions before buying:

Your home is an emotional purchase – you care about how it makes you and your family 'feel'. It must fit the checklist of personal criteria that you and/or your family have. You may even pay a bit more than you'd originally planned for the property, and that's okay because you really want it! You have the expectation that it will eventually go up in value but that's not the main reason for the purchase. This property is your home – it's part of who you are.

Here is a checklist of common requirements many people want their home to have:

- ☐ Does it have enough living space, bedrooms and bathrooms for the family?
- ☐ Is the backyard fenced?
- ☐ Is it near local cafés and shops?
- ☐ Is it close to public transport?
- ☐ How far is it from work?
- ☐ Does the property need to be renovated now or eventually?
- ☐ Does it have a swimming pool and/or a big backyard?
- ☐ What type of parking is available?
- ☐ Is it close to the children's schools?
- ☐ Does the neighbourhood feel friendly and safe?
- ☐ Is it close to family and friends?
- ☐ Does the property feel like 'home'?

The bottom line is that this personal checklist is not formally written down; most buyers carry it around in their heads. Yet the checklist determines whether or not enough criteria are met to ensure that the buyer (or buyers) will be happy in this property. Once the property is purchased, it changes from being a house to a home. That's a very important distinction. Home is where you invite family and friends; it is your own unique, intimate and personal space.

On the other hand, an investment property is a logical purchase. It's bought for 'investment reasons', so the figures, such as rental returns and projected capital growth, are of primary importance. The expectation is that over time the price will double, ideally within ten years. It will always be a house, *not* your home.

Here are some buying criteria that may be considered when an investor is purchasing an investment property:

☐ What is the projected growth of the suburb where the property is located?

☐ What are recent sale prices of properties in or near where the property is located?

☐ When did the property sell previously and for what price?

☐ What is the current purchase price?

☐ How much deposit and stamp duty will be needed?

☐ What are the projected mortgage costs?

☐ What is the cost of insurance?

☐ What is the current rent or projected rental return?

☐ What is the estimated cost of property outgoings?

☐ What are the estimated monthly costs to let and manage the property?

☐ Will the property be negatively or positively geared?

☐ What is the exit strategy for the property?

As you can see the primary concern is how much money you're spending to get in and what the projected return will be over time. The figures make it more of an impersonal process. You set out to stay within your budget, and there would need to be a good reason for you to exceed it.

You may purchase an investment property that you wouldn't personally live in, yet a tenant will rent it. The investment property may not be located near your home. You'll speak impersonally about your investment property to your mortgage broker, bank manager, managing agent and accountant. It will always be a property on a spreadsheet, where you analyse expenses and income – it will never be your home.

Of course when you buy your home, you need to know your numbers too, and which price range to look in, but that's not the driving force. And when you view investment property, you'll want to know the layout and physical features of the property, but that's often to confirm the projected returns.

Be clear about the type of property you're buying up-front. If it's your home it's an emotional buy. An investment property is a logical purchase. Either way, clarity saves time and money, and gives you the added bonus of having the certainty that you're on the right path. Break this rule and you risk losing time, money and, most importantly, becoming part of a negative, frustrating process that is far more painful than it ever has to be!

My mission is to show you how buying property can be a fun, joy-filled process for everyone involved.

When using the buying strategies I've laid out in this book, you'll also discover that creative transactions often don't fit a traditional structure. No longer is gold, in the way of property bargains, found lying on the ground. You have to create them and I'll show you how to sift and sort to find the gold.

You'll need to find out what both parties are trying to achieve and what problems need to be solved. The answers may not be apparent at first glance. The answers only come to you when you ask the right questions – and only when you ask the right questions and listen to the answers can you structure the transaction. And often, there will be numerous ways to put it together – not just one!

Buy and fold

Buy and hold *should* work. In theory, it *does* work. In theory, anyone can profit from property ownership if they follow the rules. Simply buy a property that historically increases in value, hold onto it for a few decades while it grows in value, and receive your profit when you sell. But for some reason this works out very differently in practice than in theory. Imagine if there was another way – a way to profit from property *now* instead of waiting decades?

People buy property for all kinds of reasons and they are mostly emotional, not logical. Sometimes people want to avoid a pain or make a gain. Some of the common reasons that people buy property are that they:

- crave the security of not having to move every year (emotional)
- are sick of making their landlord rich (emotional)
- are tired of paying 'dead rent' (emotional)
- believe buying a house will save a rocky relationship (emotional)
- think they're getting a bargain (emotional)
- have an accountant who says they need a negatively geared property (logical).

Ask yourself whether you're buying a property for emotional or logical reasons. There is no right or wrong answer to this question. You just need to be very clear about this before you buy. I teach my students that **you must know your exit strategy before you go into the entrance of any property transaction.** Before you buy you must know the answers to these four questions to get clarity:

- Do you plan to live in it?
- Is it an investment property?
- Is it for long-term capital growth?
- Is it for cash flow?

Traditionally, if your exit strategy is to live in the house, it'll be your home first, and an investment second. Your own home is usually an emotional purchase. Whether or not it has long-term growth or potential cash flow if you move out at a later date are not the primary reasons you're buying it. You're buying it because of how it makes you and your family feel.

If your exit strategy is to have an investment property, it is a logical purchase. Your motivation and reason for buying is to make a profit.

The *way* people buy property has as much to do with whether they profit from it or not as *what* they buy does. But most people don't put much thought at all into which way to buy – they just do it whichever way their accountant tells them to. My belief is that it's important to be crystal clear and focused about the reasons *why* you are buying a property. At the same time, you need to listen to and feel your gut instincts – you need to balance your feelings with the facts.

Be careful not to project your personal motivation and reason for buying or selling onto your buyer or seller, because everyone buys and sells for their own reasons, and everyone's reasons are different.

Buying property costs money, and holding property costs money. Everything seems to be going fine and then, 38 months or so into their 30-year mortgage (on average), people often find themselves stressed out of their minds, and struggling to scrape enough cash together to feed the kids. I hear versions of this same story all the time. The traditionally accepted system just doesn't work. Something needs to change – and it needs to change fast.

BUY FOR THE WEALTH OR THE CASH FLOW, NOT FOR TAX DEDUCTIONS

So, let's take a closer look at how it's all *supposed* to work. Then we might get a few insights into why it doesn't, and we'll see what we can do to turn the tables and create our own financial freedom.

Accountants like negative gearing because they see the benefits of the tax deductions. Negative gearing means your monthly mortgage payment will always be more than your tenant's rent, for around 12–16 years, and you'll have to pay the difference personally every month. How much of a pain is that for you to make a financial gain?

Negative gearing was always intended to be offset by high capital growth property, which is traditionally located within ten kilometres of the centre of any capital city. Property this close to the city traditionally has higher capital growth than property further out into the suburbs. Many people have negatively geared property to take advantage of tax deductions, but they forget the rest of the formula: purchase your investment property using the ten-kilometre rule. People often negatively gear for the sake of tax deductions alone – they lose real money every month to save tax, which in itself makes no sense. It makes no sense because you are taking money out of your pocket every month in order to *lose* money. But it makes even less sense if the property breaks the ten-kilometre rule, because the capital gains aren't high enough to cover the accumulated loss.

You can't have it both ways. You can receive high capital growth and no cash flow, or high cash flow and low capital growth – but not both.

I was motivated to start investing in property because I had a job I disliked. I obviously needed to make money, but I didn't want my job to be the only place my money came from.

So, I knew I needed money. But there are two kinds of money – wealth and cash flow. Wealth grows over time, and cash flow pays the bills each month. The master wealth plan is to buy things that grow in value, and hold onto them while they grow. Buy and hold. Traditionally that's where the wealth money is.

But no one can live on wealth immediately. It's like farming. We need a machine that gives us *cash flow* in the meantime so we don't starve while we're waiting for the crop of wealth to grow. Here's how it works:

- Generate some cash flow (aka 'get a job').
- Fund some 'wealth' property with some of the cash.

- Live on the rest of the cash.

- Let the wealth grow until there's enough to live on.

Usually the kind of property that grows in value actually costs money each month to hold onto, so we're negatively geared. Which means we need cash flow again, not only to keep ourselves fed and clothed, but also to keep holding the house while it grows in value.

Now, when I say 'cash flow', I mean income. More precisely, *net income*, which means there's money left at the end of the month. The most common form of income comes from a job, but it's also very common that a job will leave you with a fair bit of month left at the end of the money.

So if buy and hold works, but has a few problems associated with it, and cash flow solves all these problems, then cash flow is the answer.

Here's what happens in a typical, average life: go to school, play sport, study hard (or not), get a phone (money out), get a job (money in), get a car (money out), move out of home (money out), fall in love (like it or not, money out), get a house (money out), get new furniture for the new house (money out), have kids (money out), renovate (money out), work hard to get a promotion because you need the extra money (money in), get a new car (money out), kids need school/clothes/braces/iPods (money out), marriage counselling because you're at work too much (money out), get an investment property for the tax breaks (money out), health issues (money out), midlife crisis (money out), divorce (money out), fall in love again (money out) … etc, etc, etc.

In that whole equation, there's only one thing bringing money in – your job. And it seems like the list of things that take money out just keeps getting longer and longer.

That's the common way – the old way. And the old way doesn't work for long, just look around.

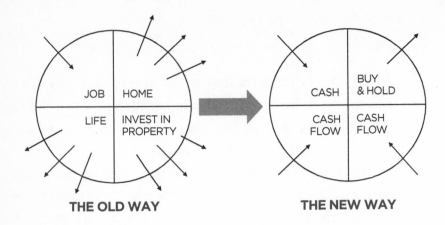

THE OLD WAY   **THE NEW WAY**

We need to change to the second picture – the new way. Yes, your buy-and-hold property that grows in value will cost money to hold onto. But if you have a few cash flow machines that have more money coming in each week than goes out, then holding onto that property doesn't cause problems. The problems come when your job is the only thing you depend on to bring money in.

So here's what I learnt to do early on:

> **Use some properties to generate cash flow,**
> **and use other properties to grow wealth.**

Of the different kinds of investments that grow in value, I prefer property. Property always made more sense to me than shares or other things. I like the fact that people always need somewhere to live, and I can do things to directly impact the value. Sure, property prices rise and fall, but shares are just pieces of paper, and can potentially disappear altogether. And I've never lost a house yet – it's always right where I left it the day before!

WHAT PEOPLE *REALLY* WANT

When it comes down to it, people don't buy or sell property to make money, even though they may *say* that's why. They actually buy and sell for what they can *do* with the cash, capital gain and profit, and – most importantly – how that makes them feel.

I always ask what people want the money for, and the list of the most common answers is pretty short. At the end of the day we all want the same things: to relieve the pain of a problem situation, to have financial freedom, to travel the world, to spend more time with the children, to give back to our favourite charity, to live life on our own terms, and do what we'd like to do when we'd like to do it!

> **'In order to do what? And how would that make you feel?'**

How does that make you feel? This is the magic question – it's what it's all about. We're all chasing a good feeling. None of this is about logic.

Humans base our decisions on emotion and how things make us feel. People don't do anything for money. It's what the money enables them to do, and what it allows them to buy into. Money is just a tool to make them feel what they want to feel.

If we know that this is what everyone wants – to be able to do what they want to do, to feel happy, fulfilled, great and excited – then let me ask you something ...

> **Experience is what you get when you don't get what you want.**

Who's got that feeling now?

Usually no one has. But isn't this what the standard process is designed to do, to give us the feelings we want most in life? If no one's got that feeling, I think we'd better start questioning the process.

More people 'buy and fold' than 'buy and hold'.

Remember, according to the Australian Bureau of Statistics Housing Survey 70% of people who buy an investment property sell it within five years, and 47% of those who sell within five years will either lose money or barely break even.

This is a big concept shift. The old way has most people working long hours, feeling angry, living unhealthy lives, coping with marriage break-ups or drug and alcohol abuse. Escapism, stress and depression are at all-time highs. This is what the media calls 'mortgage stress', and it plays a big part in everyday life.

This is all because we can't do what we want to do, and we can't feel what we want to feel. So maybe we just need to create a different way to achieve that.

I recently helped a gentleman named Jeff turn his three negatively geared properties around from a $70,000 a year loss to a $40,000 a year profit. Any situation can be turned around. Same kinds of properties, different process. But first, he had to shift his thinking.

It usually takes around four months to sell a property the traditional way. All agents do to try to sell a property faster is discount the price. But dropping the price doesn't make the property any easier to buy, and you end up with a property that's just as hard to sell *and* you get less money for it. When price is the only thing you look at, everybody starts discounting the prices of their houses, and we end up pushing the market down. Nobody wins in that game. I see a lot of red ink around, especially when people are forced to sell for less than the debt on the property.

When someone decides to sell a house, they'd usually prefer to sell it as fast as possible. As you'll see in the next few chapters, a house that's easy to buy sells a lot faster than a house that's being sold the traditional way. Dropping the price doesn't make a house any easier to buy, but changing some of the terms does. The traditional process doesn't take this into account. This is also why price-led strategies don't work, which we'll go into in a lot more detail in the next chapter.

The old road always gets us what we don't want.

People who are buying want the opportunity to own their own home and everything that will make them feel – especially security and peace of mind. People who are selling generally want the relief from the emotional concern – and they want peace of mind too. They either want the pain to go away, or they want the gain that comes as a result of selling the property.

When we focus on what buyers and sellers really want it opens up a whole range of different ways that we can transfer properties between them.

Most people think you can only do things one way – the way their bank and accountant and real estate agent told them to do it. And they think they have to just put up with it and suffer through. They never think to question the process. But that's just one way, just one process – you can create as many different processes as you like.

In the traditional processes, nobody gets what they want. They just put up with what they get because they think there's no other way. But, as you're about to see, processes that make a house easy to buy and fast to sell have nothing whatsoever to do with dropping the price – and at last the buyer and seller can both get what they really want.

Four ways to buy at a discount

There are many ways to get a discount when you buy a house, but they're not always obvious – until you know what you're looking for. For example, stamp duty, which is normally payable by the purchaser, can be negotiated into the transaction as being payable by the seller. All my transactions are stamp duty inclusive. The seller always pays the stamp duty when I buy a house. This is a great benefit to me as the purchaser, because it means I don't need to hunt around for extra cash.

Houses are easy to buy at a discount. You just need to be aware of the types of discounts that are available, and the 'hows' and 'whys' of each. Let's take a look at four ways you can buy houses at a discount:

- the 'who you know' discount
- the 'way the transaction is structured' discount
- the 'building condition or location' discount
- the 'emotional need of the seller' discount.

THE 'WHO YOU KNOW' DISCOUNT

My father once said to me that you need to build your network of connections, and by the time you are around 40 years of age they will feed you for the rest of your life. So I always say to my students, if 2,000 people know what it is that you do, you will simply be plugged in forever and you'll always wonder how people got your phone number.

I have a friend who started a business a few years back lending money to people as a private lender. His business is only three years old and has grown quickly. I asked him about his advertising machine and he admitted that he doesn't have one. Instead of advertising, this is what he did: when he first started his business he made 30 phone calls every day for the first 90 days, without fail. He called ten mortgage brokers, ten developers and ten solicitors every day, telling them about his service. He did no other advertising at all. And his phone has not stopped ringing since, delivering a constant stream of new business.

I've been teaching this concept to my students and recently attempted to have a lunch with one of them. He came to lunch equipped with two mobile phones, one for potential buyers and one for potential sellers. To my frustration these phones just didn't stop going off during our lunch. When I asked him who was calling he said they were all new clients calling for the first time. And they weren't getting his phone number from advertisements – it was 100% word of mouth.

When I was in the USA buying foreclosed properties from the Resolution Trust Corporation (RTC), which was a temporary federal agency established in 1989 to oversee the disposal of assets from failed Savings and Loans, an asset manager once said to me that although I never was prepared to pay as much as other people, the RTC just found me easy to deal with.

The 'who you know' discount is the discount you receive when people are deciding who to work with. They want somebody who can solve a problem quickly and hassle free, and you can get a lot of discounts just by having a reputation for doing what you said you would do, in the time frame you agreed to do it.

THE 'WAY THE TRANSACTION IS STRUCTURED' DISCOUNT

My personal assistant's husband called me and asked if I could assist him in buying a property for his business. He's a mechanic and he wanted to buy a mechanic shop in Paddington in Sydney. I asked him the price of the property and he said it was $1.8 million, but he had negotiated the price down to $1.65 million. I asked him how much of the amount he needed to come up with, and he told me the entire $1.65 million. I suggested that a restructure of the transaction might be called for. I suggested that he give the seller the $1.8 million, which would make the seller happy, in return for some flexibility over the time frame in which the funds were paid. The seller agreed to take 65% ($1.17 million) up-front, with the balance ($630,000) to be paid at a rate of $50,000 per year, interest free. The bank was happy to loan

65% of the purchase price, and my PA's husband didn't need to put in any of his own cash.

A few months later he called me for more advice. The seller had found another business opportunity and wanted to know if he could receive the balance in return for giving my client a discount. The seller agreed to take just $400,000 in a lump sum so that he could get the money fast. My client simply had his original loan increased by $400,000, which wasn't an issue because the property had increased in value.

In summary he received a property for $1.57 million, without investing any cash. Had he done it his way he would have paid $1.65 million and would have had to come up with a $577,000 deposit (35% of the price), which he didn't have.

Another example of discount structuring is to recognise that the buyer's purchase expenses can be absorbed and paid by the seller. Certain taxes are charged to the buyer upon the purchase of a property. The governments that charge these taxes simply want them paid; they don't really care which party in the transaction pays them. When I buy property I often have the seller pay the stamp duty – this is a great benefit for me, because it means I don't have to come up with the extra cash to cover the duty. The handed-down custom may be for the buyer to cover these expenses, but it doesn't matter who pays them, as long as they get paid.

I also like to buy houses where the contract contains a clause that everything inside the house stays with the house, except for specified works of art and small children. This is immensely popular, as many people dislike the idea of packing to move and would prefer to leave a lot of what they consider to be 'old stuff' behind and pick up nice new appliances for the new house. I've never met a woman who, given the choice, has said 'No' to brand new Smeg appliances! When my father found out I was buying houses this way he said, 'Gosh why didn't anybody offer this to me? Do you know I've been dragging that old sofa of your mother's around for the last five houses!' And an off-the-cuff question like, 'Which car comes with the house?' has enabled some of my students to build up such a collection that I've had to ask them which business they're in: houses or cars?

Delayed settlements are also great. I've found people will delay settlement for up to 12 months if they can have access to your deposit now and allow you to move in if you agree to cover any mortgage expenses they may have over the interim period. This is priceless, because people love the idea that you'll service their home loan prior to you settling, but their home loan monthly payments are usually much lower than your new ones would be if you settled fast.

THE 'BUILDING CONDITION OR LOCATION' DISCOUNT

In your standard contract of sale, you want to have a good inspection clause built in. A good inspection clause gives you early possession of a property before settlement, where an access clause won't. Many sellers' legal representatives don't like access clauses and will edit them out of the contract. But inspection clauses won't be deleted. If I'm onselling a property, and all my future buyers can inspect it before I've settled on it, I can usually have it sold prior to even owning it, which massively reduces my holding costs.

If I plan to have any work done to a property I'm buying, I like to have it done prior to paying for the property. Sellers see this as a benefit to them, because if I renovate and improve the property before I've paid the seller for it, the seller can't lose. Either I'll buy the place at the agreed price, or if I don't settle, they will have a place worth more. I can also build my works contract into the price of the property so the building contractors are paid at settlement out of the seller's proceeds, and again, a fair amount of this being included as part of the purchase price. When you add these pieces together, it amounts to a very big discount when compared with the traditional sales option.

Building condition and location are other ways to receive discounts. I like to have a long period of time to get my building condition reports done. Then, if necessary, I sit with the seller and agree on how we are going to split the costs of bringing the property back to reasonable condition.

It's important to read the pest reports. Upon hearing that a property has a pest issue, many people simply cancel the contract to purchase and move on to the next property without digging deeper to find out what kind of pests they are dealing with and exactly where the pests are. I remember I received a big discount on a property because the pest report showed the presence of termites, which was scaring everybody off. So the seller kept dropping the price. But when I read the report it showed the termites were in the front fence and the letterbox! Not only did I get a great discount on the house but I also got to go shopping to pick out a new letterbox.

I've found that 50% of people won't buy purple houses, houses near power lines, prisons or main roads, or houses that need work. For this reason they will often be sold at a discount. On the other hand, the other 50% don't care and will buy them – they simply want the opportunity to get on the first rung of the property ladder. So why not go ahead and buy those houses at a discount and sell them on at the market price to the people who don't care about purple or power lines?

As a general rule when you're buying, look at the price range for the suburb. Break the price range into thirds. You should buy in the bottom third of the price range for that suburb, and sell in the top third of the price range. Because if you buy in the top third price range and try to sell for more than that, people won't buy because for that price they would rather live in a more affluent suburb.

THE 'EMOTIONAL NEED OF THE SELLER' DISCOUNT

The last type of discount is the emotional discount. First, we need to understand that all human decisions are based on emotion, not logic. If humans were logical, we'd all be single! People either want to avoid pain or make a gain (move from a problem to solution). This is seen when people wait and wait, hoping to achieve top dollar for a property. Then they hit a tipping point where emotions take over and they have to sell due to financial urgency, which is usually tied to emotional reasons such as divorce or a deceased estate.

An agent called me once, and his words to me on the phone were, 'I feel a discount coming your way'. When we viewed the almost-new house, the interior had been splattered with buckets of different coloured paint. I was able to guess that the couple was no longer in love and just wanted to create as much distance as they could from each other. Neither party was prepared to put any life energy into fixing up a property that might somehow benefit the other person – in cases like this, any profit that couples make needs to be split between them. Quite often people would prefer the quiet joy that comes from 'good riddance' than the plasma TV a few extra dollars at sale could buy them, and that means you can pick the house up for a good discount.

Deceased estates are often just as emotionally charged as divorce sales. I was called once about a run-down property that had been left to four brothers as a deceased estate. I agreed to meet all four brothers at the property, where some fix-up work was taking place. I asked the brothers which one of them had the job of fixing the place up before they sold it. I then congratulated him on his work, and on the fact that he was obviously getting a higher share of the profits for the work he was undertaking. He gave me a puzzled look, as he was obviously getting the same share of the profits as the other three brothers, despite his extra efforts and responsibilities. I left, but they called me back a few days later and told me they would stop the work immediately and sell the house to me as it was. Yet again, where emotions are high, so are the discounts.

FOUR WAYS TO BUY PROPERTY AT A DISCOUNT CHECKLIST

BONUS GIFT

(Value $17.95 - yours FREE)

Don't pay 'full price' ever again. Use this checklist to save $10,000s on your next property investment. You can even avoid paying the 'dreaded' stamp duty.

NOTE: These are strategies that no other property educator will tell you about.

Download your FREE checklist of the **Four Ways to Buy Property at a Discount** here:

www.howtobuyahouseforadollar.com/free-stuff

How to buy a house for a dollar

Did you know that Luna Park in Sydney was purchased from the New South Wales Government for $1.00? It's true. The government sold the 99-year Luna Park lease to Multiplex for $1.00 in 2005.

Did you also know that:

- Twenty-nine ABC Learning Centres were sold to the charity Mission Australia for $1.00 each in 2009

- *The London Evening Standard* newspaper in the United Kingdom was sold for £1.00 2009
- The USA magazine, *TV Guide*, was sold for $1.00 in 2008
- The Dutch bank ING purchased Barings Bank for £1.00 in 2009
- Chelsea Football Club in the United Kingdom was sold for £1.00 in 1982

THE AUSTRALIAN ✹

ABC Learning centres sold to charity for $1 each

Natahsa Bita   *April 23, 2009*

FAILED childcare centres reliant on taxpayer funding have been sold to a charity for $1 each.

Mission Australia paid a token $1 each for several of the 29 ABC Learning centres it bought from the collapsed childcare chain's receiver, PPB, industry sources told *The Australian* yesterday.

Ex-KGB spy buys UK paper for £1

Russian ex-KGB agent Alexander Lebedev is to buy the *London Evening Standard* newspaper for the sum of £1.

The paper's publisher – the Daily Mail & General Trust (DMGT) – said it had agreed to the sale of a majority interest in the paper to Mr Lebedev.

The billionaire businessman is believed to have made an offer for approximately a 76% share of the paper.

OpenGate buys TV Guide for $1

Macrovision sells struggling magazine for cheap

BY CYNTHIA LITTLETON

A dollar won't buy you a cup of coffee these days, but it will buy you TV Guide. No, not an issue of the weekly mag – those go for $2.99 – but the entire publication.

Yep, $1. The eye-popping sale price was disclosed Thursday in a Securities and Exchange Commission filing from *TV Guide* owner Macrovision, which revealed it had struck a deal to sell the magazine to venture capital firm OpenGate Capital on Monday (*Daily Variety*, Oct. 14).

October 16, 2007

Luna Park may reap millions for $1 land buy

Sunanda Creagh, Urban Affairs Reporter

A property developer stands to make an estimated $7 million by selling the lease on a piece of Luna Park land that was bought from the State Government for only $1.

Luna Park Sydney, a business controlled by Multiplex, has advertised that the 99-year lease to the land plot known as Site C – a harbourside cliff-top spot in Glen Street, Milsons Point – is for sale to anyone interested in building a restaurant or office block there.

In a 2005 deal, the Government sold the 99-year lease to Luna Park Sydney for $1 on the condition the company invest in the maintenance of the fun park.

You can transfer debt from one company to another for a dollar. Why charge a dollar or a pound? Because it shows that 'some consideration' has been paid. It could be any sum, as long as it shows that something of value has been handed over in payment. So if companies move debt around for a dollar when they buy and sell each other, why can't we apply the same process, systems and formulas to houses?

We can! Here's how it works. They're transferring the debt to the new owner, and the asset goes with it. And they pay the one-dollar fee to stick the paperwork together. The company is sold for a dollar, and the new owner takes over the old debt. It's much easier to transfer the debt and the assets to a new owner than it is to set up a new company from scratch. Especially in times when banks aren't giving out new loans very readily.

Companies, in one respect, are just like houses – they're made up of a cash bit and a debt bit. And, just like houses, nobody wants to keep the debt bit. They only like the cash bit. So the old owner moves the debt bit across the table to its new owner, and they seal the paperwork with a buck.

When we get to the strategies section, you'll see exactly how to put this concept into action for yourself. But first, I'd like to show you all about selling to ensure that you make a profit when you sell the property you buy for one dollar.

ALL ABOUT SELLING

When you're selling a house you want to be able to sell it as fast as possible and for as much money as possible. Unfortunately, traditional processes usually result in the house sitting on the market for many, many months while the agent keeps dropping the price, because that's the only way they know how to attract buyers. There's nothing worse than being stuck in limbo, waiting for what seems like an eternity, and being unable to buy a new house until your old house sells.

Let me tell you something that deep down, you probably already knew: *dropping the price doesn't make a house sell faster.*

In many cases, dropping the price only creates a financial loss for the seller and doesn't create a financial benefit to the buyer, because they still can't purchase the property.

Let's say a seller has a $600,000 house and the agent asks them to drop their price to $550,000. Does this make it any easier for someone to buy? Let's do the maths:

To purchase a $600,000 property, you'll need $120,000 in cash as a 20% deposit. For a $550,000 property, you'll need $110,000 in cash. When the seller drops their price, the difference of $10,000 is not going to add that many more new people to the pool of available buyers. If you don't have $120,000 in your bank account you certainly aren't going to have $110,000. But as the seller, you have just lost $50,000 trying out a price reduction to find a buyer.

In these next chapters, I'll show you how to keep your price and still sell your properties quickly, by simply changing the formulas.

The truth is that when you make a house *easy* for someone to buy, it becomes easy (and faster) to sell. When you make a property easy to buy, and make the decision easy for the buyer to make, then you can sell a property faster and for more money than you ever thought possible.

Two components are needed to buy a property: finance and cash. In reality, in today's market there is very little available finance and what is out there is rapidly becoming more expensive. Just imagine how much easier it would be in this time of reduced bank lending if you could simply service the loan already obtained by the seller, and didn't have to get a new loan. It would be quicker and simpler to put a property transaction together, with fewer forms.

Over the years, my students and I have found that marketing a house based on how easy it is to own far outweighs selling a house on its features and benefits.

For example, if a property is marketed as 'No bank loan required to own this $600,000 house', it will sell much quicker than a comparable house that's marketed as having 'Shiny new taps and fresh paint'.

People sell property for one of two reasons: to move away from the debt bit or to get hold of the cash bit.

Sometimes when people sell a house, it's not that they want the house to go away, it's that they want the obligation of the payments (the 'debt bit') to go away, because it's affecting their lifestyle. Or sometimes, it's because they want to capture their 'cash bit' in order to pay out other debts, invest elsewhere for a higher return, put cash in the bank, or buy another property.

So if you understand that moving away from the debt bit or receiving the cash bit are the two primary motivations why people sell property, we must ask ourselves if this is the most efficient system.

The last time we updated the property system in Australia was 1919, the same year that Qantas flew its first canvas-and-stick airplane in Australia. Now passengers fly in the Airbus A380, so maybe it's time we modernised the vehicle we use to buy and sell property too.

By the end of the next few chapters you'll see how to find eager buyers *and* get the price you want for your property. You'll have everything you need to sell your house in a week, so that you can get free and clear of your old house, have the money in your pocket, and be ready to move forward with your life.

Why you can sell in a week

No one is useless in the world ...
who lightens the burden of it for anyone else.

– Charles Dickens, *Our Mutual Friend*

Harvey Norman doesn't sell big-screen TVs and surround-sound stereo systems. And 7-Eleven doesn't sell snacks and slushies. They both sell convenience. It's all about the convenience, not the price.

7-Eleven doesn't compete on price with the local supermarket, even though it sells a lot of the same items. At 7-Eleven, you'll often pay 25%, 50% or even 100% more for the exact same thing. And you won't even question the price because it's closer to home and open 24/7. Pure convenience.

Harvey Norman provides convenient finance terms, such as 40 months interest free, which enables its customers to have a big-screen, high-definition movie experience in the comfort of their own home today, without saving up the money first. And if Harvey Norman didn't offer convenient payment terms (that is, if people had to save now and buy later), it would lose more than half its sales.

Buy now, pay later.
No deposit, no interest.
Pay less for cash.

You've heard it all before. But, what does any of this have to do with property? Everything.

We've all accepted the idea that we'll pay more for convenience. We've all become familiar with the idea of paying less for cash. And we're all comfortable with the idea that we can buy now, pay later, with no deposit and no interest. Because we know it happens all the time.

These ideas have seeped in, and are living happily in the back bit of our brains, and they can unconsciously impact how we buy and sell property as well as household electronics. Now, let's see if we can make the impact of these ideas a bit more conscious and a lot more profitable.

Harvey Norman makes more sales because it's happy to accept delayed gratification. Of course it wants all the money for what it's selling, but it doesn't need it all *today*.

Most property sellers don't need all their money today either. They only want the cash now because they've never been shown any other way to profit. Most of the time they end up getting a lower price *and* they have to wait four months or more before the house

It's about convenience, not price.

sells. If they knew they could get their full asking price, and get it this week, do you think they'd be happy to receive some now, some later? You betcha!

Most buyers aren't happy to pay the full price, because at the back of their mind there's a quiet little voice saying, 'Pay less for cash'. So, thinking that cash is the only way they can pay, and price is the only variable, they have no choice but to lowball. But if we take *price* out of the equation and replace it with *convenience*, things change dramatically.

IF I MAKE A HOUSE EASY TO BUY, IT BECOMES EASY TO SELL.

When it comes to property, the convenience is in the terms. By changing the terms so they solve a buyer's problem, we can make the house easier to buy, and significantly increase the number of people who are able to buy it.

If you want to make a property sell faster, you need to get more people interested in buying it. When lots of people are interested in buying it – and are *able* to buy it – it will move like lightning. It's basic supply and demand. More buyers = higher price = faster sale. So the big question is …

How do we get more buyers?

Sydney has the highest property prices in the country at the moment. And Sydney house prices are the furthest out of reach for most people, too. Let's look at an example:

To buy a house with a $500,000 price tag (which is a common price in a place like Sydney), a buyer would need a $100,000 (20%) deposit, and another $22,000 to $25,000 for stamp duty and legal costs. How many people in Australia and New Zealand have a lazy $125,000 sitting in a cheque account for a rainy day? Less than 1%. Which means that with the traditional system, over 99% of people couldn't buy that property, just because they can't cover the cash expense. Whether they qualify for a mortgage or not doesn't even come into the picture.

But what if the seller said, 'You only need to give me $20,000 cash today, and the rest of the deposit later'? A heck of a lot more people would have that kind of money to get started, so there would be many more potential buyers. The property would sell faster, simply because it would be easy to buy.

I define a potential buyer as someone who would be able to afford the monthly payments if they bought the house (and by *afford*, I mean the monthly payments would be no more than 30% of their monthly income). To be taken seriously by a bank or lender, potential buyers need to be able to do three things:

- afford the monthly payments
- come up with a deposit
- qualify for a loan.

I focus mostly on the first factor, because if that's solid, the other two can be figured out in a whole variety of ways, using flexible terms. The last two can often be a little more challenging for a lot of people who are buying the traditional way.

So, we've already looked at the number one hurdle for most potential buyers: the deposit. Now, let's take a look at the other big hurdle for potential buyers: qualifying for the loan.

At any given time almost half of all Australians, even if they have a deposit in their pocket and oodles of money coming in like clockwork every month (even if they have the tax returns to prove it), can't get a loan – so they can't buy your house. There are many reasons for this, and it's mostly to do with the way the bank system and credit system evaluate things.

You'll notice I didn't say they couldn't get a *big enough* loan – these are reasons that good, reliable, financially viable people can't get *any loan at all.* This is why dropping the price is a useless strategy for these people. It hurts the property values for the entire neighbourhood, and it doesn't make your house any more affordable, attractive or

I solve problems. If they don't have a problem, I'm not their guy.

easier to buy. The people who could buy it at $550,000 are the same people who can buy it at $450,000, and they still don't want it at any price. The people who have a deposit and a loan have options. The people who don't have a deposit or a loan have problems.

TOP TEN REASONS WHY HARD-WORKING PEOPLE CAN'T QUALIFY FOR A BANK LOAN

10. Missed payment on one mobile phone bill

9. No consistent savings record

8. Not enough deposit

7. Too many footprints on their credit report

6. They're a new immigrant

5. They're self-employed

4. They've had too many different jobs

3. They've moved house too many times

2. They have too many houses, and can't get any more credit

1. Their credit file got tarnished during a divorce

In the 'good old days', your loan was approved or denied by a bank manager – an actual human with some perspective and discernment. Nowadays, banks use computer modelling, with rules and statistics.

The computer can say 'no' even if you've had perfect credit all your life – a *single, solitary unpaid bill* that happened years ago during the craziness of a divorce is reason enough to deny a loan application today. Moving house or changing jobs twice in three years, or being self-employed, apparently means you're unstable and makes an applicant unsuitable for a loan by the computer-approval process. Even more common – especially if you don't know what order to do things in while you're putting in your loan application – is that the very *act of applying for a loan* can put unwanted hits on your credit file, which then destroys a perfect credit history and results in loans not being approved. None of this relates to real people and real life.

So here are *my* criteria for potential buyers:

- They have to have a burning desire to own their own home.

- They need to be able to afford the monthly payments.

- They need to have 'get started' money and a problem I can solve.

In my live training workshops we go into all the details of how to conduct background checks, which paperwork to use, and things to look for to attract top-quality potential buyers. But it all comes down to meeting these three criteria. Do they really want it? Can they afford it? And how motivated are they to solve their problem?

I want people who can afford to make the payments on a bank loan but simply haven't been able to get one. And there are lots of them out there. If they have problems, I can solve them. And if I can take the pain and the problem away, and give them what they want, they'll give me what I want by default, every time.

todaytonight

The home loan for battlers

REPORTER: Michelle Tapper
BROADCAST DATE: September 16, 2002

Saving for a deposit on a house to get a home loan can be the hardest step in trying to own your own home but hardworking families who have been rejected by the big banks have been left frustrated, bewildered and hurt.

Liz and Mike Newstead saved for years to raise a $10,000 deposit for a home loan.

"It was a catch 22. Every time you saved up enough deposit the prices of property would go up again," Mr Newstead said.

"It's very heartbreaking. The dream home was going further and further away," Mrs Newstead said.

"All I wanted in life was just to own my own home to give my children something for the future."

When the Newsteads' eldest daughter was struck with leukaemia, they spent their deposit on her treatment.

Mr Newstead had to quit his job as a travelling salesman and their dreams of owning their own home were dashed.

"Even though we were able to save about $5,000 back as a deposit, it still didn't meet the banks' criteria for savings history," Mr Newstead said.

"They said we didn't have a steady saving history and that we hadn't been in work for long enough," Mrs Newstead said.

Catherine and John Tippler also received a similar spiel.

As a self-employed plumber, Mr Tippler was repeatedly turned down for a loan by banks. "Over the years we would have gone to over ten of them for sure. They just won't even look at you, won't give you a chance," he said.

Rick Otton is the founder of We Buy Houses, a unique organisation helping families break through the financial barriers to home ownership. Mr Otton says he will give almost anyone a loan and find them a house.

"A lot of people who are self-employed, or they're new Australians, or don't have the deposit requirements, or don't fit within the bank guidelines can buy homes through We Buy Houses," he said.

"We can help you buy a house if you've got a minimum deposit of $10,000." If you qualify for the first home owners' grant – a $7,000 government rebate – you only need to save $3,000.

"They don't have to go through the hoops that they have to go through with the banking system," Mr Otton said.

"We are a stepping stone that allows people to buy their own home and after a year or so, refinance into the standard banking system," he said. For Mr Newstead, the higher interest rate was not a concern, as it helped him get his foot in the door of the housing market.

"We didn't mind paying the higher interest rate because it was the only way that we would actually be able to buy a house now and not have to wait for another 20 years to try and save the deposit," Mr Newstead said.

Last February the Newsteads bought a four-bedroom home from Mr Otton and they refinanced at a lower interest rate with a bank earlier this year.

"I love the fact that we're paying off our own home rather than spending the rest of our life renting, paying dead money," Mrs Newstead said.

In April this year Catherine and John Tippler found a four-bedroom fibro home that needed renovating for $168,000.

"To buy a house worth $160,000, to go to a normal lender you need 20 percent deposit, which is $32,000, compared to our $5,000 that we needed to go through with We Buy Houses," Mr Tippler said.

We Buy Houses has helped almost 40 Australian families in the past three years and some 300 families in the United States, where they have been in business for almost ten years.

"We negotiate hard to buy houses at a discount and then we just find people – of which there's a whole market share of people – who are unable to qualify for homes tomorrow and we make our houses available to those people," Mr Otton said.

Now these battlers are forging new frontiers.

"We bought it for $161,000 and it's worth between $200,000 and $250,000," Mrs Tippler said.

So if you're one of thousands of families snubbed or rejected by the banks because you don't have a huge deposit or credit history, We Buy Houses might just be the solution you need.

"Now the banks are chasing us, saying 'would you like a credit card?'" Mr Newstead said.

"So it's just really different to be treated differently by a bank when before you just couldn't even get them to give you a free rubber stamp, so it's a good feeling."

SELLING PROPERTIES THE QUICK & EASY WAY CHECKLIST

(Value $25.95 – yours FREE)

Don't pay outrageous real estate agent fees and sell your property quicker. This checklist will show you how. Discover everything from how to advertise on a shoestring to asking the right questions.

Download your **FREE Selling Properties the Quick & Easy Way Checklist** here:

www.howtobuyahouseforadollar.com/free-stuff

Everyone loves a bargain

People get excited about bargains. But you don't just find bargains lying in the street or sitting in the real estate agent's window. Bargains are the result of solving problems, and problems are opportunities. So what you need to look for are opportunities to create bargains.

For some people, a bargain might be a lower price, or a honeymoon interest rate, or accepting the deposit in six equal payments instead

Don't go looking for a bargain – bargains are created, not found.

of needing it all up-front. For most people it's not about the price, it's about how the price is paid.

To create a bargain, you need to know what the buyer really wants and what problem they need to solve. And you need to know what the seller really wants, so that means you need to know what problem they need to solve, too.

For example, I like to ask agents if they have any houses where the seller owes more money than the property is actually worth. One time an agent had a house that wasn't selling. The seller had a debt of $465,000, but the house was only valued at $460,000.

I suggested that if the seller was happy with the idea, then I could take the house at the above-market price of $465,000, and I'd pay the mortgage on the seller's behalf. The seller and the agent were both over the moon.

The seller was able to walk away from the house without paying another cent, which was great for him, because he hadn't been able to see any way to solve his problem before. And I was able to walk into a three-bedroom brick home by babysitting an existing loan, which was great for me because I didn't need to qualify for a bank loan or come up with a deposit.

As you can see, what may have looked like dirt in the shop window actually turned out to be nuggets of gold – for both parties – as the transaction came together. The profit is *always* in the way you pay for a property, not the price you pay.

A bargain is a transaction that solves everyone's problems at the same time.

When you create a bargain, everyone gets what they want. When the buyer gets what they want – the opportunity to turn your house into their home – they get excited; when the seller gets the price they want and it's sold tomorrow, they get massively excited as well.

When you make your house easy to buy, it's easy to sell.

SELL THE EASY WAY – STEP BY STEP

Use flexible terms to make it easy for people to buy.
    Know which problems you (the seller) need to solve:

- ☐ What's the market price for houses just like this in the local area?
- ☐ How much money do you need right now?
- ☐ How soon would you need the rest?
- ☐ Which terms could you be flexible about?

Know which problems you can solve for a buyer:

- ☐ No deposit?
- ☐ No bank loan?

Find eager buyers who have those problems and:

- ☐ Structure the terms to solve their problems.
- ☐ Talk it through and agree on a transaction together.
- ☐ Use the right paperwork.

So, we've seen how having flexible terms puts many, many more people in a position to buy your house ... but how do you find these people? Or how do they find you? Everyone knows where to find the local Harvey Norman store to solve their entertainment problems, because Harvey Norman has a great marketing strategy – it might not be the fanciest marketing, but it lets everyone know where to find a store, loud and clear.

Marketing is important, but I don't mean the glossy, shiny advertisements that everyone's become accustomed to. I mean a simple, out-of-the-box marketing process that stands out from the clutter. It creates a point of difference and lets people know you exist. Marketing is about differentiating yourself and standing out from the crowd. If the crowd is shiny, go ugly! Ugly signs sell houses! People know where to find my students and me so that we can solve their property problems the same way they find out about bargains at a garage sale:

With a cardboard sign on a stick!

Sure, it sounds tacky and ugly, but if you advertise your house like you would advertise a garage sale, people *will* find you.

When people see a shiny, graphic-designed, full-colour ad in the newspaper or on a sign out the front of your house, do they think, 'Look, I could get a bargain here', or do they think, 'Ugh … real estate agent. I'm paying full retail'? If there's one thing that a sign on a stick does, it's scream BARGAIN!

Many of my students have tested this idea over and over again. And the results are always the same. Even in the poshest suburbs, a shiny ad gets fewer phone calls, while a cardboard sign on a stick gets the phone ringing off the hook. Often my students will go to the local hardware store and buy a corflute sign and scrawl on the back with a thick black marker. And the phone starts to ring!

The back bit of our brains already knows that:

'shiny expensive sign' = 'real estate agent' = 'full-price retail'

AND

'ugly scribbled cardboard sign' = 'garage sale' = 'bargain'

Ugly screams bargain!

So using that knowledge is the first step. The second step is knowing what to put on the sign and what NOT to put on the sign. First, you have to make sure you don't sound like a real estate agent ... so no marketing hype, and no listing the features of the house.

What your sign SHOULD have on it is simple ... you have to solve your potential buyers' problem. If the problem you're solving is that they don't have a deposit, say 'No deposit' on the sign. If the problem you're solving is easy finance with no bank qualifying necessary, write 'No bank qualifying' on the sign. Keep it short and sweet and simple.

People often overcomplicate this with advertising and copywriting jargon, but you really just want to keep it simple. We obviously go into a lot more detail in our live training, but really, you've got all you need to get started right here. Solve their problem, write your first name ('Call Rick' – it makes it personal) and make the phone number big and clear so they can read it. This will get the phone ringing, and you'll get to start solving some problems and selling some houses.

Why discounting your price is the most common selling mistake!

What 99% of people do when they want to sell a property quickly is discount the price. But when you discount the price, you'll find your neighbour, who is also selling their house, discounts their price too. Then all the other people in your neighbourhood start discounting the prices of their houses, and you end up with everyone fighting to have the cheapest house and creating a losing market.

Dropping the price doesn't bring in more buyers, because it doesn't make it any easier to buy.

Not only that, but price makes negotiation a nightmare. The seller wants the price high, and the buyer wants the price low. They both can't possibly win that game at the same time, so somebody always ends up unhappy. In a price war, everyone loses.

If not price, then what?

Rather than dropping the price of your property, one way you can increase interest is to make it easy to buy your property. You can also look at ways to make your property more enticing to buy than your neighbour's property.

Everyone has money; they just don't have it all today.

You can tailor the transaction to solve specific problems. As long as the buyer and seller agree on the transaction, the paperwork can be created to support it.

And most of the time, the paperwork actually already exists.

What you do is really only limited by your imagination and the problems you're trying to solve. To open your mind to what's possible when you change the terms instead of the price, here is a short list of some of the terms that my students and I have changed in real transactions, with real people and real properties:

When you are flexible about the time frame in which your price may be paid, it means more people are able to buy, and are willing to pay your price.

- ☐ No deposit
- ☐ Reduced interest rates lower than mainstream lenders
- ☐ Some now, some later
- ☐ Pay off the deposit in instalments instead of up-front
- ☐ Rent now, credited to purchase later
- ☐ House and car package
- ☐ House and furniture package
- ☐ Discount the buyer's interest rate, not the house price
- ☐ 'Sweat equity' (the 'handyman special') – do a renovation as a deposit
- ☐ Pay instalments to the seller instead of to the bank
- ☐ Stamp duty paid by the seller not the buyer

And many, many more ...

Keep it short, sweet and simple

14

Just suppose ...

People make decisions based on feelings, and then they justify their decisions (to their spouse or accountant) with logic. When you phrase everything as a question, you help them to step through their own discovery process – and you actually help them to understand their own problem in a new way, so they can make a real decision and take action on it.

First you have to listen to them – ask questions and get them to do all the talking. Just like a doctor doing their diagnosis. When it's time to give them your prescription, you can't tell them what to do – nobody likes being told what to do. But you *can* float an idea by them.

Knowing that people make decisions based on feelings, when you add these three key phrases to any idea you suggest, you'll find that they work wonders.

'Just suppose ...'

This phrase sidesteps any resistance to the idea you're suggesting, because you're not telling them what to do, you're just floating an idea.

'... if we could do this, this and this ... you could do that, that and that ...'

This is the idea you're suggesting – the meat in the 'Just suppose ...' sandwich. It's important that you listened when they were doing all the talking, because the 'that, that and that' in the sentence above is what they told you was most important to them. And most people will be willing to do something (your idea – the 'this, this and this' bit) if it gets them what's most important to them (their 'that, that and that').

'How would that make you feel?'

This question disconnects them from logic and connects them with feeling, which is how people make their decisions. When they're in logic mode, no decision is actually possible. Only when they're in feeling mode can they make a real decision and move forward – 'How would that make you feel?' gets them there.

It's important to suggest just one part of the idea at a time, because the brain can make one small decision at a time and move forward. I call it shutting the gate – you need to wrap each part of the idea in a 'Just suppose ...' sandwich, get agreement, shut the gate, and move on.

'Just suppose ...' moves people from confrontation to collaboration. Instead of seeing you as their opposition, it brings you both to the same side of the table looking at an idea together. Try it! It works like magic.

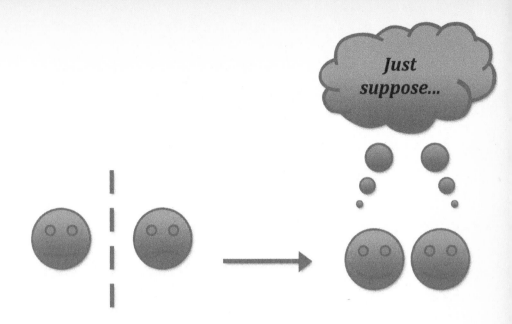

*One way gets results and
the other way gets resistance*

You need to remove the concept of confrontation or conflict from the negotiation. If you can move physically to the same side of the table, all of a sudden you're on the same side – you're no longer in opposition. Now you're looking at the problem together and you can move forward towards a solution as a team.

Shutting the gate – one-point negotiation

If a woman asks her husband, 'Do you want to go scuba diving in Bali in February?' He'll most likely say, 'No, I can't get the time off work'. It's not because he doesn't want to go – it's because it was an intimidating question. There was too much information in the question, making it too difficult to process. In fact, it was really six (or more) questions hidden in one:

- Do you want to go on a holiday?
- Can you get leave from work?

One way gets results and the other way gets resistance.

- Do you want to go in February?

- Do you want to fly for more than six hours?

- Do you want to go scuba diving?

- Do you want to go to Bali?

The human brain can only make one simple concrete decision at a time. When you have a multi-question question like that, it's overwhelming, and it's just easier to say no.

The key to shutting the gate is to ask one question at a time, get agreement on it, then shut the gate and move on to the next question. Just get commitment to one point at a time, and keep moving forward. Each time, the gate clicks shut behind each question.

So, something like this might be more effective:

Wife: 'You know how you've got six weeks' leave from work?'

Husband: 'Yeah.' (*Click.*)

Wife: 'Have you got anything on in February?'

Husband: 'Nope, it's quiet then.' (*Click.*)

Wife: 'February's quite warm, isn't it? Great time to get some scuba diving in?'

Husband: 'Sure.' (*Click.*)

Wife: 'Did you want to stay in Australia, where it's quite expensive, or fly to an island somewhere?'

Husband: 'An island would be great.' (*Click.*)

Wife: 'I know you don't like to fly more than six hours away. What island could we get to on a short flight? It has to be Bali, doesn't it?'

Husband: 'Guess so, yeah.' (*Click.*)

Wife: 'Great, I'll book the flights.' (*Click!*)

It works exactly the same way with any conversation you have. You need to make it easy for someone to make a decision by confirming one simple point at a time, shutting the gate, and moving forward.

And yes, Jane and I are probably heading to Bali in February!

How does it work with houses?

Here's how it might go with a buyer (after you've listened to them, you know you're talking to the right person, and you've done your diagnosis, obviously):

You: 'How soon are you looking to move in?'

Them: 'This weekend would be great.' (*Click.*)

You: 'How much rent are you paying now?'

Them: '$450 a week.' (*Click.*)

You: 'How much up-front money would you have to get started?'

Them: 'Around $5,000.' (*Click.*)

You: 'Up to ... ?' (*Pause.*)

Them: '$8,000.' (*Click.*)

You: 'But no more thaaaaan ... ?'

Them: 'Actually, we've got $8,200.' (*Click.*)

You: 'Just suppose we could create a way for you to move in this weekend, and your same rent payments could be going towards owning your own home instead of being dead rent. How would that make you feel?'

Them: 'Great, let's do it!' (*Click!*)

Taking them through this process, one step at a time, is far gentler on the sensitive decision-making muscles in the brain. Most people get overwhelmed when trying to make big decisions, so make the decisions bite-sized instead. Remember, speed kills deals – they need time to get their head around what you're talking about. Make the process easy for them and they'll reward you for it.

'JUST SUPPOSE' QUICK REVIEW

When you combine all that you've learnt so far:

- you know that people buy and sell to **feel** better
- you know it's about **convenience**, not price
- you know to buy for **cash flow**, not tax deductions
- you know that **bargains are created** not found
- you know terms are **flexible**, so any transaction is valid
- you know the **transaction** always comes first, and the paperwork second
- you know the four ways to **buy at a discount**.

When you combine all that, WOW! You're *way* ahead of the curve, and we're only halfway! In the next few chapters you'll:

- get to know the **five core strategies**
- discover which **words** work like *magic*.

And you'll find, when we get into the paperwork in the next section, that once you know these things, you *can't* stuff it up. It's simply impossible! But we're getting ahead of ourselves. First, let's negotiate!

THERE IS ANOTHER WAY

Marketing and negotiating are simply about three things:

1. being unique and getting noticed

2. solving people's problems

3. talking to people – saying the right things, in the right way, to the right people at the right time to get what you *both* want.

It starts with structuring a transaction that benefits the other person first, then attracting the right people who have problems you can solve.

But before we go on, I just need to warn you: *marketing defies logic*. With marketing and negotiation you're dealing with humans, you're not dealing with logic. Some things work and other things don't, every time, like clockwork. Why? We don't know. They just do. We see the same patterns happen over and over again – so often that it's impossible to argue with them.

It's also all about what the *other person* thinks, not what we think – while *we* think it's about us or about logic, we can't move forward. Humans are emotional creatures – we do wacky stuff that doesn't make sense. I've been dealing with people for a long while, and I've noticed patterns that get results. If you ever find yourself thinking, 'Well **that** doesn't make sense,' just remember:

You're not dealing with logic; you're dealing with *humans*.

Humans will drive to the gym to get fit then spend ten minutes driving around the car park trying to get the closest park to the front door. That's not logical!

You've probably heard this before – 'It's not what you say, it's how you say it'. Well that applies here as much as anywhere. And the way to say it is *simple*.

That's right – I said simple. Here's why …

People trust, and can do, simple. Keeping it simple is the key – the less you say the more you make. So, the way to make sure you're not intimidating is to:

- stop wearing suits and looking so 'professional'
- use 'mums and dads' language, not jargon
- ask, ask, ask … don't tell!

If someone feels intimidated, they're not going to be relaxed and they're not going to feel comfortable moving forward. If they feel like you're smarter than they are, they're going to want to talk to their solicitor and accountant and get advice from their family. But if they feel like they're smarter than you, they'll relax and feel free to give you more information. They'll also feel more comfortable around you, they'll feel like they're getting a bargain, and they'll want to seal the deal fast, before you go get advice and change your mind.

Some of the 'mums and dads language' terms we use are so that we don't seem intimidating. Others we use because people just like them better and respond to them better. A contract is a scary formal legal document, but people handle pieces of paper every day. Nobody has a deposit, but everyone can find some 'getting-started money'. Nobody feels equipped to 'renovate', but people love to 'fix it up and clean it up'. Nobody wants to 'buy' anything, but everyone likes to 'own' stuff. You might say it's the same thing, but saying it one way gets results, and the other way gets resistance. Which one do you want?

A lot of people seem to think that insulting somebody's house will make them drop the price, so they point out everything that's wrong

How to use 'mums and dads' language

PROFESSIONAL JARGON	'MUMS AND DADS' LANGUAGE
Mortgage	Loan
Buy	Own
Vendor	Seller
Equity	Cash bit
Mortgage	Debt bit
Instalment contract or terms contract	Some now, some later or pay it over instalments
Lease option	Rent and buy or rent-to-own
Deposit	Getting-started money or move-in money
Serviceability	How much a month?
Assume the loan	Babysit the loan
Renovate	Fix it up or clean it up
Contract	Paperwork or forms
Buying from	Working with
Selling to	Transfer to/from

with it. I don't know anyone who likes being told that something of theirs is awful, so here's what I do: I tell them it's the best home I've been into. It's the greatest thing I've ever seen. If I fall through the floorboards as I walk through the front door, I come up saying, 'I love your basement!'

It's marketing again – I want to stand out and be remembered. And I want to be remembered as a nice guy who will take care of their home.

I always look at properties at six pm, when the tenants are there, so I can find out what I need to know. I say to the tenants, 'Congratulations, I may be buying the place. What's the first thing you want me to fix?' They'll tell you everything!

With sellers, I'll ask unusual questions, and sometimes they'll get great results. If there's a termite problem, I'll ask, 'What's the termite discount?' And I'll often ask, 'So, which car comes with the house?' This works about 5% of the time. I don't know why it works, it just does. One of my students has ended up with 11 cars just by asking this question!

At the end of the day, with any negotiation, you just need to uncover the story. When they feel comfortable enough with you, they end up saying, 'Mate, can you get me out of this problem?' When that happens, they know you're on the same team and then you can craft a solution to their problem and create the paperwork to support it.

No one will move forward while they feel intimidated – but if they feel like they're smarter than you, they'll buy now. They need to feel like it's safe to tell you anything. As long as they believe you're no smarter than them, people will always do business with you.

Don't be like the IT person who talks to you in total geek-speak. We all do the same thing – we smile and nod as if we know what they're talking about, but really, we just can't wait for them to leave.

So stop looking 'professional' and speaking in jargon – because it's costing you money! I don't wear a suit – I wear relaxed, casual clothes. And that's okay, because people like to deal with real people, not companies – you'll make money because you're real, not because you're polished. And while you're at it, strip out the sales language. Say, 'I'm not too sure, could you tell me how that works so I can help you further?'

You've got to believe before a buyer or seller will believe. And you need to make sure everybody's singing from the same song sheet. You do this by seeking clarification after every point is explained, and every suggestion is made. Ask the question ... **'Just suppose we could do *this* ... so you could do *that* ... how would that make you feel?'** Because their FEELINGS will determine their actions.

DOWNLOAD YOUR FREE SUCCESSFUL NEGOTIATING TIPS SHEET

(Value $27.95 – yours FREE)

As my gift you can download a FREE copy of my **Successful Negotiating Tips Sheet**. Post it on your wall so you can review these tips often and they'll become as natural as brushing your teeth!

This is your chance to become a 'knock out negotiator' creating win/win property deals.

Download your **FREE** copy at:

www.howtobuyahouseforadollar.com/free-stuff

FIVE CORE STRATEGIES

O nce you get familiar with the ideas we've looked at so far, there's no limit to what you can do with them. Pretty much every time you're presented with a problem, you'll be able to find a creative way to solve it so that the buyer and the seller **both** get what they want.

IS THIS YOU?

- You want to own your own home but you haven't saved enough deposit and/or your credit isn't perfect.

- You are a first homebuyer and you believe that owning a home is almost an impossible dream.

- You want to create a home-based business allowing you the freedom and flexibility you can't get with your nine-to-five job.

- You are a property investor and you want to keep buying property, but the banks won't extend you additional credit.

- You own a negatively geared property and you can't afford to keep making the payments.

- You own a property and if you sell it you will have to write a cheque at settlement because you owe more on it than it's worth.

If you can relate to any of the above scenarios, this section is all about the solutions you've been looking for.

In this section we're going to review the most common core strategies that I use, and that my students use, over and over again. Don't think you need to learn all of them, or even understand all of them. The truth is, you can use any one of these strategies, get good at it, and then repeat it over and over again to achieve more than you've ever imagined.

When one person is buying a house from another person, there are two overall 'bits' of the payment that need to be taken care of in every transaction: the up-front bit (deposit) and the balance. The strategies you're about to see will show you different ways to take care of the up-front bit, and different ways to take care of the balance.

You'll see all the strategies in their most basic form – but remember, you can mix and match many of them like Lego® pieces.

While it's true that whenever two people come together anything goes, there *are* common problems that come up over and over again. The would-be first homebuyer who has a great income, but can't save up a deposit; the empty-nester who is asset rich and cash poor; the couple who got into investment property to grow their wealth, but found that negative gearing killed their lifestyle and their peace of mind.

It comes down to three fundamental problems, how do we buy, sell and hold property without sending ourselves broke or losing peace of mind in the process?

Once you get your head around this, the creative alternatives and possibilities really are endless. We'll go through a few of the most common scenarios here so that you can start to get familiar with the basic building blocks. It's like learning to play music – first you need to learn to play a few of the tunes, then you can choose to keep playing those, or you can compose some of your own.

FUNDAMENTAL MONEY PROBLEMS

Buying problems

☐ You can't save up a big enough deposit.

☐ You can't get approval for a loan.

Selling problems

☐ No one will pay the price you want.

☐ You can't sell fast enough.

Holding problems

☐ Your mortgage payments cost too much and you can't maintain them.

☐ You need to generate extra income to service your mortgage.

When it comes down to it, there really aren't that many money problems that our strategies need to solve. Solving money problems is easy. Where the creative part comes in is finding ways to *use* the strategies in our toolkit to solve *real-life* problems. Real-life problems create money problems, but when you solve a real-life problem, you replace the money problem with a sense of relief and peace of mind.

When you offer flexible finance terms, you can finance the whole house or just the deposit. By offsetting a little of the buyer's expense, you can put a honeymoon period on interest rates like the banks do. Or you can offer a grant like the government does. These finance strategies will make your property more attractive, and help you to sell it faster without needing to drop the price.

HERE'S HOW IT WORKS

Let's say someone is trying to sell a house worth $400,000. Different problems can arise depending on how big their loan is. People only ever sell for one of three reasons:

- to get their hands on the cash bit (money bit)
- to stop paying the debt bit (mortgage payments)
- to solve a 'people problem' (divorce, inheritance and so forth).

Houses A, B and C are all worth $400,000. But each house has a different loan amount against it, which means each seller has a different motivation – a different reason – for selling. When you ask why they're selling, they'll all say, 'We need the money'. But you need to dig deeper than that. Which money they need (cash bit, income, or relief from mortgage payments), and *why* they need it is very different in each case, so they'll each need a different solution.

Why are the owners of House A selling? The mortgage payments aren't a hassle, but something happened in their life and now they need to get their hands on the $20,000 cash that's sitting in their house. And they need it as soon as possible.

A traditional real estate agent would charge an advertising fee and maybe get them access to their cash (or less) in four months (or more).

If I could write them a cheque for $20,000 in 60 seconds and then have paperwork systems handle the rest of the details, do you think they'd prefer that? Of course they would, because they need to access the cash bit now. They'd get instant peace of mind, *and* their $20,000 cash.

Some people, like the owners of House B, don't even have a cash bit. They just want the debt bit to go away so it stops killing their marriage and their joy. There's no cash bit in this equation.

So, I can go in there with a couple of forms, and start to look after the debt bit for them. I don't have to give the sellers any money in exchange for their house; I just need to babysit their loan. How much money have I just used to buy my first home? None – and I'll end up with a payment of about $3,000 a month, and my first home. Or I could use another strategy to turn that payment into positive cash flow for myself (as you'll see in the examples in the next chapters).

The point is the owners of House B didn't have to lose money and sleep while they waited for four long months. I could make their whole problem disappear immediately with the right paperwork system, so they could have instant peace of mind and stop paying their mortgage payments.

Why are the owners of House C selling? Obviously it's not about the cash bit, because there isn't one. Even if they sell the house today for the market price of $400,000 they'll have to find an extra $50,000 to settle their debt. They want the pain and the problem to go away. Just selling the house won't make the debt bit disappear. But my systems will.

You can see how this problem is also created when someone in House A or B discounts their price. The lower they drop the price, the worse it gets, because when they drop the price it doesn't reduce their debt. But they don't even have to discount it much before there's trouble. This is exactly how the old system creates more problems than it solves.

Normally, sellers want me to pay their mortgage for them. But I have to remind them that I'm here to find a solution to their problem, not just to transfer their problem from them to me. So we work together to find a solution – which is to find someone who wants to live in their house more than they do.

So, I can babysit the loan with a form, just like I did for Houses A and B, but to solve the $50,000 dilemma we'll have to add another step. I'd either find a rent-to-own buyer, or do a handyman special, or use one of the other cash flow strategies that work equally well to turn negatively geared property around, as you'll see in the following chapters.

Instalment
contracts

Instalment contracts, also known as terms contracts, have been around for a very long time. Much of the Blue Mountains, Newcastle and even north Sydney were originally sold using terms contracts. They always become popular when bank loans are hard to get, and were very popular after the war and up to the early 1970s. Even today they are used to transact a lot of country property.

With a standard house sale both legal and equitable title are transferred to the buyer prior to the borrower repaying the loan, and the loan from a bank or financier is secured by way of a mortgage, which allows the lender to sell the property if the borrower defaults and the loan isn't repaid. With an instalment contract the *seller* provides the buyer with the loan – usually under better terms than offered by banks – but only gives them the equitable title, holding onto the legal title (the ownership) until the borrower has paid out the loan. In most cases the borrower sells or refinances the property prior to the loan term expiring, and repays the loan, at which time the legal title is transferred to them. I explain the process to buyers by simply asking them how much of the purchase price of their car I would need to give them before they signed over the car registration. They always say, 'All of it', to which I answer, 'Good, then you'll be all right if I feel the same way about my home'.

In a standard purchase and sales agreement, contracts exchange and settlement takes place in 30 to 90 days. With an instalment contract the settlement is delayed up to 30 years, but the seller receives the sales proceeds over time in the form of monthly principal and interest payments, just like a bank does with a mortgage. A sale has still taken place, but how long the seller is willing to be paid instalments for, how often they should be paid, and the interest payable is what's known as instalment payment terms.

Although instalment contracts are generally written for the same term as a bank loan (25 to 30 years) they tend to last for less time than that, as people sell or refinance early. Just like a bank loan, buyers will incur legal and applicable stamp duty expenses similar to that of a standard home purchase. Because buyers are committing to the idea of owning the property today, they tend to be happy to pay a larger deposit to the seller, and a deposit of 5% is not unusual. Less than one in ten instalment contracts fail to complete.

I remember my first transaction using an instalment contract. It was in Australia in the year 2000 – a time when not many solicitors were familiar with the process, because instalment contracts had been dormant for a while.

I was told the concept would not work here because most people could get a bank loan and anyone who couldn't get a bank loan wouldn't be able to pay the applicable stamp duty anyway.

I bought the first property for $94,500. I advertised it as a home you could own without a bank loan. I had around 15 potential buyers to pick from, and I onsold it to a couple for $106,000. The husband, having worked for 20 years in the air force, was changing careers, and the banks would not give him a loan at that time. He was happy to pay 2% higher than standard variable bank rates over 25 years, because he thought it was a fair exchange for being able to buy a property with just a $6,000 deposit.

Like most people would, the new owners painted the place and cleaned it up a bit, and then they refinanced 18 months later when the banks decided that his new job was secure.

INSTALMENT CONTRACT VARIABLES

Because I wanted all my buyers to seek legal representation for their purchases, I needed to find solicitors who were familiar with instalment contract documents. I went from solicitor to solicitor and almost all of them gave one of two responses:

- Yes, we can – but we haven't done these for over 30 years.

- No, we don't do them.

When I thought about this, it made sense, because the last time these documents and processes were popular was in the mid-1960s.

A common way to start using instalment contracts is by simply purchasing a property at a discount, either in the traditional way or otherwise. Buyers using instalment contracts will pay around 7% above market price in exchange for having the opportunity to buy and being able to have the finance attached to the property, so in order to increase the profit you need to buy at a discount.

I recently bought a property where the sellers were moving overseas and the property wasn't selling fast enough. The house was on the market for $430,000, but I was able to buy it for $400,000 by putting down a 10% deposit and securing a 90% loan for the balance at 7% interest, payable over 30 years, which worked out to be $2,395.09 per month.

Many people would choose to renovate to increase market value, and in the early years I would have spent time making the house pretty for sale. But now I don't bother, because the people coming in are not looking for a choice of houses, just the opportunity to *get* one. Now I simply believe in making the home easy for someone to own, which has the same effect, and saves me from having to read up on how to use a hammer! I re-marketed the property at $460,000, which was 7% above the market price.

I advertised the property using a classified ad with the headline, '*No bank qualifying to own 3 bed home*', and as people called I simply asked them:

- When would you be ready to move?

- What sort of work do you do? How much do you earn?

- How much money do you have to put towards the home?

The buyers were doctors who were new to Australia. They had large incomes but had not been in the country long enough to be approved for a loan by Australian banks. They gave me a $25,000 up-front deposit, and I gave them an instalment contract for the balance. The transaction we worked out was $435,000 at 8% for 25 years, which put their payments at $3,357.40 per month, giving me a positive cash flow of $962.31 every month ($3,357.40 less $2,395.09 = $962.31).

Then, because they wanted to own the property faster, I reduced the loan term by five years, which increased my monthly cash flow and also saved them interest.

As the new owners of the home, the instalment buyers pay all insurances, maintenance and taxes. As the lender I pay no ongoing expenses – I just sit back, having collected $25,000 up-front to help offset my original $40,000 investment in purchasing the property, and collect $11,547.72 a year cash flow, which is a cash on cash return of approximately 77% on the $15,000 cash I still have invested. When the buyers refinance (which 99% of people will do within five years), I'll receive around $35,000 in backend profit.

Instalment contracts are very 'set and forget' and you can even automate them by having all payments collected by real estate agents, who check that all payables and outgoings are handled, and simply transfer the positive cash flow into your account monthly. They even print up a report for you at tax time. Like low-doc loans, the market will pay a higher interest rate, similar to that of low-docs – somewhere between 2% and 3% – and you can decide how long you want the loan to be, remembering that the shorter the loan term, the higher the buyers' payments, and your monthly cash flow, will be.

When qualifying people you ideally need to ensure that their payments to you will not be more than 33% of their gross income. A good rule of thumb is that the average person can buy a house that costs around four times their annual income, so if they earn $100,000 they can afford a $400,000 house.

Instalment contracts are great because they allow time to pass, giving people the chance to let small credit impairments disappear off their credit history. And because you're providing an actual loan to them, it makes it easier for them to get refinanced at a later date, because any potential new lender will be able to check their previous payment history.

In the unlikely event that a buyer defaults, the process is the same as a bank's process of foreclosure, and your solicitor can handle this, as it is a standard process. But this is a rare occurrence – usually, a chat and a cheque goes a long way towards moving a buyer who has trouble making their payments out. Then you're free to move a new buyer in.

In summary, the seller becomes the banker, and as such makes the decisions about who gets the opportunity to own the home on the easy terms offered. Then the property will sell fast at its full retail price. You simply use a solicitor to create sales papers for you, and get them to punch in the numbers you dictate.

THE '10:10'

Twenty years ago, 70% of homes in Australia were owned outright. Today, over 38% of homes in this country are still owned outright with no debt against them. When someone sells one of these properties, it's not usually about getting their hands on the cash bit, or about ending the pain of the debt bit. Usually it's to fund a lifestyle instead of being asset rich and cash poor.

Most people think they need to sell their house and put the money in the bank or into some managed fund or investment scheme to create an income. But with the 10:10, it's a lot simpler than that. With the 10:10, you (the buyer) just pay 10% more to the seller over ten years. Here's how it works:

Me: 'Why are you selling?'

Seller: 'I need the money.' (*That's what they all say.*)

Me: 'What do you need the money for?'

Seller: 'I need to retire, and I need an income stream to live off.'

Me: 'You're asking $400,000 for the house. I'll give you $440,000.'

Seller: 'Sure, what's the catch?'

Me: 'If I agree to give you $440,000, that's 10% more than you're asking for, would you have some flexibility on the time frame over which you receive the funds?'

Seller: 'I suppose. How much flexibility?'

Me: 'Well, just suppose I could give you the full $440,000 in monthly instalments over ten years, giving you regular monthly cash flow. How would that make you feel?'

Seller: 'How much would that work out to?'

Me: 'Could you punch in the numbers?' (*I give the seller the calculator*) '$440,000 divided by ten years, divided by 12 months a year. How much is that?'

Seller: '$3,667.'

Me: 'So that's $3,667 per month. How soon would you like the first cheque in your bank account? I can give it to you right now. How does that make you feel?'

Seller: 'Sure! That's great.'

Of course, you can come to arrangements with a different number of years, and different instalment amounts, but it's the same basic framework. Sometimes they want to calculate how much they'd get if they sold the house and put the money in the bank – my transaction is better for them. Sometimes they ask why I'd pay more. I tell them that I'm willing to pay more for the flexibility of paying it off in instalments – just like at Harvey Norman. Everyone knows you pay less for cash.

Here's how it works out for me: at the end of ten years, I've paid $440,000 and I own a house outright. At the end of a normal 30-year mortgage on the same house, I would have made over $1 million in payments. I like the 10:10 strategy better. I win and the seller wins ... and the bank *doesn't* win for a change.

A student of mine was working with a pensioner who wanted to sell his house. Now, when a pensioner sells a house for $435,000, it's not about selling the house ... it's about what selling the house will do for the pensioner. Here's how the dialogue went:

Student: 'Why are you selling?'

Seller: 'I need the money.'

Student: 'What do you need the money for?'

Seller: 'I need money to live on in retirement.'

Student: 'What will you do with the money from the sale?'

Seller: 'Dunno, probably just put it in the bank.'

Student: 'So, are you more interested in getting the most money for this house or the most income from this house each month when you retire?'

Seller: 'Well, as much income as possible every month.'

Student: 'How much interest can you get at the bank?'

Seller: 'About 5–6% I guess.'

Student: 'Would you rather get 5% or 8%?'

Seller: 'Well, 8% of course.'

Student: 'And if you were getting 8%, would you really care which bank it was with?'

Seller: 'No, of course not.'

Student: 'Why don't you let me buy this house from you? I'll pay you close to 50% more than the bank was going to give you, so you'll get more income every month, and we'll get your legal representative to put all the paperwork together for us. How would that make you feel?'

Seller: 'That'd be great. Why didn't anyone ever offer me this before?' *(They all say that, too.)*

So, the seller won because he got an income stream paid to him monthly. And as a buyer, my student got to buy the house, with no money down, and he didn't have to fill in any forms for a bank loan. He could just move in and simply start making monthly payments.

Are you starting to see the possibilities now? How many doors could this open up for you? Understand that I'm just giving you the basics here – these strategies are pretty cool, but they're just the fundamental scaffolding, so you get an idea of what's possible. Like I said before, once you get your head around this, it's amazing what you can do!

Take a look at a couple of the transactions our students have done:

Rob – bankrupt in Deception Bay, QLD

This guy was going bankrupt when he found me. I paid $2,500 of his arrears payments, and put legal paperwork in place, which said I would guarantee to babysit his loan until other people bought the property. The loan debt was $178,000, and I onsold the property on an instalment contract for $250,000 to an air conditioning guy. He then spent $50,000 on the place, did it up and increased the value by $120,000. I got a deposit of $10,000 up-front, and agreed on monthly instalments. After two years he cashed out, and I made a profit of $72,000 on the backend. Now he's got the place on the market for $370,000.

Up-front deposit: $10,000
Cash flow: Instalment payments of $497 per month

Backend profit:	When the buyer refinanced after two years, I received the remaining $250,000, giving me a backend profit of $72,000

Brett – lots of calls from Taree, NSW

My wife and I spent a few days in the country town of Taree, looking for a house to buy and then onsell for a profit. We bought a place for $125,000 with a six-week settlement, and access to the property for four of those weeks to put signage up and show people through.

We used the normal yellow signs that said, 'No bank qualifying, for sale by owner, low deposit, $325/week'. We put ads in the local paper as well.

We put signs up and started driving back to Sydney, and the phone started ringing before we even hit the freeway. We got a lot of inquiries from a lot of people on welfare who didn't qualify as buyers. We onsold it to a first homebuyer with a $10,000 deposit, plus the $7,000 first homebuyer's grant, which was paid up-front. They bought the house for $152,000 on an instalment contract with payments of $325 a week. And they paid out a lump sum of $100,000 just 12 months later.

Up-front deposit:	$10,000 cash deposit + $7,000 first homebuyer's grant
Cash flow:	Instalment payments of $325 per week
Backend profit:	When the buyer refinances, there will be a backend profit of $27,000

Deposit finance

This is a strategy where the buyer can qualify for a loan but is either short on their deposit, or doesn't have one at all. Deposit finance is also called 'Second Mortgage Carry Back' by solicitors, and here's how it works: I suggest that the buyer gets a bank loan for as much as they can borrow. I'll lend them whatever they can't borrow and I'll usually mirror the same terms that the lender offers.

For example, if my buyer can get a loan for 90% of the purchase price at 7% over 30 years, I will lend them the other 10% at 7% over 30 years. Although I don't have to mirror the main loan, I find it makes it easy for buyers to understand – I call it the 'same same' loan. I don't worry about underwriting these loans, because if the buyer can qualify for the first loan with the bank, then they are certainly good enough for me.

I have two rules for deposit finance. The first rule is that the buyer *must* borrow enough in the first loan to pay out any mortgage I may have on the property, otherwise my lender will not pass the title to the buyer's new lender.

My second rule is that the 10% must represent a percentage of profit not capital, so if for some reason I never receive it, I don't lose any of my money.

As a seller, I simply offer to finance the buyer's deposit over a period of time, which can be payable monthly with interest or as a lump sum sometime further down the road. This enables potential purchasers to buy your property with no cash deposit, which allows you to sell your property very quickly for full retail price, with no discounting. Some sellers don't require all of their funds from the property up-front. This strategy works well for them as it enables them to sell their property faster, and for a greater price, to a larger pool of potential buyers. By accepting delayed gratification they can realise a faster sale and get more money. When I buy houses I find this is a good strategy, as it is one that agents can get their heads around. It is affectionately known as the 'some now, some later'. And when I buy properties I have my 'some now' price, and I have my 'some now and some later' price.

Recently, I met with a seller who needed to sell quickly in order to spend time with his sick father on the south coast. After prolonged discussion, which mainly involved me listening, I learnt that he was an electrician and would leave his employer, but was hoping to grab odd jobs down the coast.

I said to him that I could buy his house today, and that I had a 'some now' price and a 'some now, some later' price.

He asked me what my 'some now' price was, and I told him $320,000. He said he couldn't make that work. Then he asked me about my 'some now, some later' price, and I told him I could get him $320,000 now, and another $80,000 paid to him as an ongoing income stream to supplement his income while he was with his father. We agreed on $80,000 payable to him at the rate of $500 a month until paid in full, or a future date when the balance of the $80,000 would be paid out in one cheque. This is a popular strategy, as sellers would prefer an ongoing income stream rather than discounting the price of the property for cash.

If you want to get sellers to carry the finance on your deposit next time you buy a home, ask this simple question …

'If I can get to the price you want for the home, do you have some flexibility around the time frame over which you receive the funds?'

You can never pay too much, only too soon.

Negotiations should never be around the price paid, but the *time frame* over which the price is paid.

Ben – the Winnebago deal

I call this the 'Winnebago deal', because this guy was selling his house in Craigmore, SA, to buy a Winnebago, but I didn't know this at first. We were negotiating how much money he'd take now and how much he'd take later. He was definitely open to flexible terms, but the whole time I was struggling to figure out what he really wanted. As soon as I found out that he wanted a Winnebago, we got the catalogues and looked them up online. He was so excited! He was in his mid-60s, and he'd decided it was time to drive around the country and live off his pension. And he also wanted a little extra cash to help with maintenance and repairs on his Winnebago.

When I started doing property transactions, I connected with a few accountants and finance brokers. Interest rates were on the rise at the time, and the only people buying properties were investors. So each time I got a house, I'd send a few photos, and they'd broadcast it to their clients. The accountants and finance brokers helped source investors interested in buying the houses I found, and the buyers never had any problems getting finance.

So, I onsold this house to an investor. The house was valued at $290,000, and the owner owed $110,000 on it. The Winnebago he liked cost $75,000, so he took $203,000 up-front, which covered his loan and the cost of the Winnebago and left him with $18,000 in the bank to cover repairs and maintenance. We even got a cheque made out directly to the Winnebago dealer. The investors then rented the house back to the guy on a three-year lease.

He was very happy to wait the three years for his 'deposit' – the $87,000 balance – because he was so pleased with the transaction.

Seller's profit: $18,000 cash + Winnebago
Student's profit: $23,000

Rob – no deposit in Wyoming, NSW

Knowing what I do, a couple asked if I could buy them a house. They had no deposit, but they said they could get this house really cheap. It was an unadvertised mortgagee-in-possession property on the central coast of NSW, which was selling for

$160,000 plus stamp duty, so I borrowed the money on a seven-day short-term loan for a fee of $5,000.

The property was valued at $215,000 and I onsold it to the new owner (the guy who had asked me to buy it for him) for $213,000, plus stamp duty. He gave me an up-front deposit of $8,000 and got a bank loan for $160,000. He still owes me a deposit of $47,200, which he's paying back over a 30-year term with interest, and he'll probably refinance and pay me out in a couple of years.

Up-front deposit: $8,000 cash deposit

Cash flow: Instalment payments of $363 per month

Backend profit: If the buyer refinances before 30 years, I'll get the rest of the $47,200 deposit that has not yet been paid off

Handyman special

People hate renovating. But they love to 'fix it up' and 'clean it up' – there's a market full of people who just *love* doing this stuff! There's also a market full of people who want to own their own home but don't have a deposit. What if their elbow grease could be their deposit? Then they could turn *my* house into *their* home.

The example I'm going to use to show you how the handyman special works was featured on the Channel 7 TV show, *Hot Property*. This house was like House C in the Five Core Strategies chapter. There was more loan than house, and I was helping the seller fix her loan problem. You see, the house was a mess and although it was saleable to an investor at $242,000, it had a $280,000 debt on it. This situation is becoming quite common these days. It's known as an upside down loan – there's more loan than house, and the owner can't sell the house through the conventional real estate agent system because there's no sales commission available. And even if they *could* sell the property that way, the seller would have to come up with a cheque for $38,000 to pay out the difference. So we need to think outside the square to fix this problem, because the conventional way simply doesn't work in this situation.

Valuations showed that if the house was cleaned up and fixed up, it would be worth $340,000 after the renovations. So a 10% deposit on the renovated house would be $34,000, with the remaining 90% coming to $306,000. The quotes I got for renovations came in at around $34,000 as well. No structural work – but just about everything else you could think of, including a new bathroom and kitchen.

So, here's how the transaction came together:

Seller	Me	Buyer
Problem:	**Solution:**	**Problem:**
Loan of $38,000 more than house value.	I babysit the $280,000 loan with a paperwork form.	No deposit.
Just wants the loan to go away.	I find a buyer.	Does renovation, costs $3,000 + elbow grease.
House is sold.	I sell for $340,000 with a sweat-equity deposit.	Receives $34,000 'sweat equity' credit.
No more mortgage payments: $280,000 debt is completely paid off.	I get $306,000 cash and pay $280,000 debt.	Gets 90% loan for $306,000.
	I get a $26,000 profit.	Owns their own home.
		Property is worth $340,000 after renovation.

It's all about how to buy a house with no money, and solve other people's problems at the same time. Here's another example of how it works:

A real estate agent called and offered me a house he couldn't sell because it had previously been occupied by an elderly lady and 40 cats. The smell of urine was quite pungent, and as a result I was able to obtain this property at a price that was quite a bit under market. As a sidenote, the day I inspected it I had a student come along with me, and he almost started vomiting from the smell when the front door was opened. The agent's comment was, 'Maybe I can drop a little more off the price'.

Now, I could either clean the property up and do a renovation myself to increase the value of the house before I sold it, or I could create an opportunity for somebody else. If I was to do the renovation myself it would mean learning new skills, which would cost me money because of time lost due to my lack of experience. And there's always a chance that I might not renovate the property in a style that's to other people's liking.

It was very easy to find someone who was short on a cash deposit, but had the skills and desire to renovate the property. The cash required to buy a house these days is one commodity a lot of people just don't have – but a lot of people have the desire and the ability to do the work.

A carpenter named Scott had been unable to qualify for finance because he was self-employed. And although he had problems getting a bank loan because he couldn't prove his income, he was keen to work on the property and use his own 'sweat equity' in lieu of putting down a cash deposit.

We walked through the property together and agreed upon a schedule of works that had a total value of around $30,000. Instead of Scott paying $30,000 cash, he just needed to agree to complete a schedule of works. When the work was finished and approved by me, his deposit would be considered to be paid.

Scott finished the work quickly because he was connected to other tradespeople. His $30,000 worth of sweat equity increased the value of the property by $100,000. Upon selling the property to Scott I was able to realise the profit between buying at wholesale and selling at retail. And Scott received the profit from improving the property to a higher standard. Scott made more profit than I did, but I did nothing and had time free to profit elsewhere. I'm always happy to leave some profit in the transaction for the next buyer.

Carrying back the finance for a period of time is attractive for a buyer. Buyers will often pay full retail price for a property in exchange for having the opportunity to have the finance attached to the property on purchase. Making life easier for the buyer and having the up-front deposit received in the form of sweat equity (which improves the property) also guarantees that the buyer will follow through with the purchase. It's very rare for someone to renovate a property and then simply walk away from the transaction, because by the time the renovation's done, they're invested – emotionally and financially.

I've found that having the potential buyer complete the agreed works prior to moving in works well with this strategy – the dream of home ownership keeps the paint brushes moving! I put a lockbox on the property, which provides the buyer with unlimited access to complete the work, but if beds are found in the property, all bets are off.

It's not just a house anymore; it's their home!

The standard of work is normally superior to a contractor's standard as well, because people are making a statement about their own home, which is a far greater motivation for them to do quality work. But I always insist that plumbing and electrical work is completed by a licensed tradesperson.

A SOLUTION FOR THE BUYER WITH NO DEPOSIT

I was recently called by a lady who simply wanted to move on. She was happy to accept my price based on the fact she could simply hand in the keys to the front door and leave.

When I asked a real estate agent to inspect the property he not only refused the listing, but also wished me luck in trying to sell it, because the house was a mess – there was a lot of rubbish in it, and it smelled.

I found a young married couple who could qualify for a home loan, but like many young people, they could not save a deposit. I bought the house for $236,000 and made it available to them for $279,000. Their sweat-equity deposit would be $30,000 and they could make monthly payments to me for the balance at bank interest rates. They called in all their friends to help them out, and cleaned out and fixed up the house for a material cost of around $10,000. They saved on materials by buying at auctions, and their labour cost, being sweat equity, was free.

In their mind they got a saving of $30,000, with a raw cash investment of only $10,000, and when they refinanced, the property was valued at $345,000.

I did nothing, and made just over $40,000 profit.

I always let the buyer pick the time frame over which they will complete the work. This way they are working to their schedule, not mine. If I need them to work to a shorter time frame, I simply ask them, 'Is that the best you can do?' I like to see a schedule of works as part of the paperwork that is created, and I also like to walk through the property with the buyer beforehand, simply to get a feel about them and their ability to get the work done.

When you use this strategy, buyers will always go the extra mile to make your house become their home, and they want it to look as good as possible when they're finished. One of the other reasons buyers love the handyman special is that they can use sweat equity as a deposit and then make monthly instalments to me in much the same way as they would to a bank. Later, when they refinance with a bank, they usually don't need a deposit, so it's a great work-around for when people have no 'starting up' money.

My students and I find that there are many variations of the handyman special, because it's a strategy used to solve people's problems. When we create tailor-made solutions to unique problems, the solutions will be unique as well.

Here are a couple of examples of variations on the handyman special:

Dave – single-mum renovation

I got a call from a single mum with teenage kids from Singleton, WA. She was a chef, and her work hours had been slashed by two-thirds. Her house was run down – it needed floor tiles, fresh paint, landscaping, and a new kitchen. Because she was only working one-third of her regular hours, she couldn't do it, and if she had to sell the house as it was, she would take a hefty loss.

She heard about me through word of mouth, and when she rang me she sounded like a serious, motivated seller. But I wasn't sure what I could do to fix her situation. Based on my research, if I was going to buy her house, I was going to have to offer $250,000, but houses were selling in that area for $310,000 to $330,000. I *could* fix it up, but if I did, there wouldn't be much in it for her.

This was my first no-money transaction and I had an idea how to make it work. Why not do a joint venture with her? My dad could do all the work, and we'd pay for materials and labour. We agreed to split the profits over $250,000.

It took Dad less than a month to fix the place up. We put the house back on the market, and it sold for $310,000. After expenses, I made $7,500, Dad made $7,500, and the lady got $265,000 instead of $250,000. It was great!

Up-front deposit: Sweat equity
Cash flow: Property sold in less than a month
Backend profit: $15,000 profit, split between Dad and myself

Tim – caravan and petrol money

The seller was an empty-nester – a single mum, whose kids had recently moved out of home. She was living off Centrelink payments, and had a new man in her life and they were looking to go off and do their own thing.

When I asked her, 'What do you want to achieve by selling?' she said, 'To get rid of my mortgage'. So I offered to pay her some now, and some later. I offered her $110,000 now, so she could buy a caravan and a 4WD and go travelling around Australia, and offered to pay the rest over five years, interest-free, at $100 a week, so she would also have a bit of petrol money when she hit the road. The total sale price for the house was $220,000 – and the only previous offers were low-balling around $190,000 to $200,000. Because I saved money with the interest-free arrangement, it was as if I secured a $160,000 sale price, compared with traditional purchase methods.

The house was an extremely run down, 30-year-old property. So I purchased it on a 'some now, some later' and I onsold it using the handyman special to people who renovated it over two months before they moved in. I sold it for $279,000, including a $20,000 sweat-equity deposit. The new buyers also got the $17,000 first homeowners grant, which came to me as part of their deposit. I put them on an instalment contract with a standard 30-year mortgage.

Up-front deposit: Sweat equity + $17,000 first homeowners grant

Cash flow: Instalments of $377 per week, minus outgoings of $109 per week mortgage payment, plus $100 per week cash to the seller, giving me a positive cash flow of $168 a week

Backend profit: $22,000

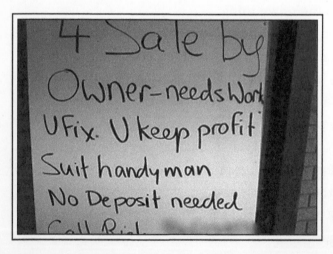

By the time the renovation's done, they're invested—emotionally and financially

Rent-to-own

The rent-to-own strategy can solve both of the major first-homebuyer hurdles: the deposit and the loan. Rent-to-own is also called a 'lease option', because the paperwork that's used to support the transaction is a residential tenancy agreement (that is, a rental lease) with an option to purchase given to the buyer. A lease option, or rental purchase agreement, is the name of the legal paperwork used with the rent-to-own strategy. Lease options are very fluid and flexible – the paperwork can be written to specify any length of time. That means that every rent-to-own agreement will be different, depending on the needs and desires of the buyer and seller. This strategy is also known as rent-to-buy, rent-now-buy-later or rent purchase agreements.

This strategy is similar to car leasing. A buyer leases a car for an agreed-upon price, and, for a specified period of time, they make a payment on the car each month. At the end of the lease period, the buyer has the option, but not the obligation, to purchase the car.

It's the same arrangement with property – when a buyer purchases a property on a lease option, it's for an agreed-upon price up-front. The buyer makes a monthly payment for a specified period of time and has the option, but not the obligation, to purchase the property – either during or at the end of the lease option period.

In fact, this is the way that the McDonald's Corporation bought its first properties to launch its global franchise empire, using almost none of its own money. McDonald's actually used the sandwich lease strategy, which you'll learn about in more detail in the next chapter.

People who can't buy a home in the traditional way will always pay more for the opportunity of ownership, so their rent will be more than what a normal tenant would pay. There is a very powerful reason why people will pay more than average rent on a rent-to-own: they see themselves as future homeowners, not tenants. Also, a percentage of the tenant's rent can go towards buying the house. The difference is you can treat some of the extra rent as forced savings that can be counted toward a deposit under the contract to purchase the house at a later date. But the forced savings only apply as a deposit for this house. If the tenant opts not to buy, then they don't get their extra rental money back, but the trade-off is that the owner sets the purchase price during the lease period, and if the property increases in value, the seller doesn't get any of the increased profit above the agreed-upon price.

A seller can use this strategy to either:

1. sell their house faster and lock in the sale price, or
2. increase the income that they get from a house.

And because the rent is higher, this strategy can single-handedly solve many negative gearing problems.

The longer the term of a lease option, the higher the percentage of people who will purchase the property; the shorter the term, the lower the percentage of people who will take ownership of the property. Instead, they'll just keep renting, and keep paying the higher rate, or they'll move out because they don't want to be homeowners.

I had a tenant who was interested in buying one of my properties, but couldn't raise a deposit. So I suggested we work together and we agreed we would change his rental to a rent-to-own arrangement, whereby he would contribute an extra $400 a week that would be credited toward the purchase price of the property. By the time he decided to buy, this extra rent ended up being 5% of the purchase price. The lender gave him a 95% home loan, and he was able to show the lender he had already given his 5% deposit to the seller (me).

He was able to find an easy, convenient way to buy, and I was able to sell the property without having to pay any of the usual selling expenses.

Another time, I bought a home unit cheaply because the banks weren't lending, and as a result the price point was too cheap. I then made the home unit available to the market at the normal market price as a rent-to-own transaction and the tenant/buyer simply paid me 'super rent', knowing that one day bank lending would loosen up, and when it did he could buy the property. As it was, he decided not to buy the unit, but sold the opportunity to somebody else who was prepared to buy it.

With instalment contracts, the buyer has already bought the house and is paying off the loan. However, a rent-to-own is a great short-term strategy to use as a stepping stone to home ownership, just like a try-before-you-buy arrangement. It's best to use instalment contracts for longer-term arrangements, as lease options should be limited to two or three years.

Rent-to-own is easy for mums and dads to get their heads around, because it's simply a residential lease, which they're already familiar with, and an option. An option is a piece of paper that contains the following details:

- The seller's name
- The buyer's name
- The address of the property
- The price the property may be bought at
- The period of time the option is good for
- The option fee and how it is payable
- The price credits for the deposit

The rent-to-own strategy gives people the choice to buy a property on a fixed set of terms, but they are not obligated to buy, so they're not locked in. Rent-to-own is ideal for:

- renovators who want to control a property for a short period of time in order to renovate it and then resell
- first homebuyers who want to get into the property market without large up-front costs
- investors who wish to control more properties without tying up cash
- sellers who want a fast exit from the market
- sellers who want to turn negatively geared property positive
- sellers who want to secure the full retail price for their property.

Of all the strategies, this is the most flexible and has the most variations – and as far as the variations are concerned, there really isn't a right or wrong way to set up a rent-to-own. The most important factor is that both the buyer and seller are in agreement.

THE POWER OF
'TRY BEFORE YOU BUY'

Many first homeowners have trouble getting over the psychological hurdle of making the transition from renting to buying. They get stuck thinking, 'What if it's the wrong house?' It's not only a bigger commitment than what they're accustomed to financially, it's also a bigger step emotionally.

Rent-to-own can serve as a stepping stone between renting and buying. First homeowners can 'try before they buy,' and lease the property for a year or two (or three) before committing to buying it.

I once bought a beautiful, south-facing waterfront property. What I didn't know when I bought it was that the house didn't get any sun, and it was absolutely freezing all through the winter. With a lease option a buyer can try the house out and find out all they need to know about it (like whether it's freezing cold all winter or unbearably hot all summer), and then commit to buying the house when they're ready.

Another way this strategy works for first homeowners is to help them save up a deposit. Tenants/buyers can pay extra rent that can go toward their deposit. It works as a 'forced' savings plan. Then after the first year or two they can go to the bank and get a loan to finance the rest of the price and buy the house.

This is how it is possible to get higher-than-market rent with a lease option. Some transactions result in the seller receiving rental amounts that are higher than what tenants would pay in a conventional rental tenancy.

A lease option is also a great stepping stone from private finance to bank finance. If someone doesn't qualify for traditional bank finance for some reason, this can be a great way for them to get into their own home straightaway. Then, a year or two down the track, after they have built up their deposit, they can go to a bank and start the traditional process of getting a loan.

PROFIT WITHOUT FEES USING LEASE OPTIONS

It's normal for people to buy a house, live in it for five or six years, then move. They buy another house, live in that for five or six years, then move again. They do this over and over again. Every time they sell they get to profit from the increase in the value of the house. But every time they buy and sell they incur all kinds of fees, rates, obligations and liabilities that come with homeownership.

Lease options enable you to get all of the profits without any of the hassles.

With a lease option, you can move into a property within a few days, so it's a lot quicker than waiting for a sale to settle. Also, the sale price is set when you sign the paperwork with a lease option. So if the price goes up, you have already fixed the purchase price and you can sell the property for a profit.

With a lease option a buyer can get control of a piece of property and do things with it before incurring all the normal ownership costs. Contractors do this a lot. They'll use a lease option to get in, use their skills to renovate and increase the value of the property, and then sell it for a profit without taking on the ownership costs up-front.

It's also possible to do a joint venture with the owner of a property. I fix the price, pay the owner rent, and I take the full profit when I sell. Here's another way to profit from the property: I could move in rent-free, renovate the owner's property over time, and we can agree to split the profits that are created when I increase the value of the house. The possibilities are endless!

NEGATIVE GEARING TURNAROUND USING LEASE OPTIONS

Based on average rental rates and average loan rates, average investment properties will usually end up being negatively geared. But we want positive cash flow. If you have a negatively geared property, getting a tenant/buyer in on a lease option instead of a normal lease can turn your cash flow situation positive overnight. A lease option is faster to put in place than a traditional property sale. On a lease option, the tenant/buyer has bought into the idea of homeownership, so they generally pay much higher rent, and they might take care of any expenses themselves.

Let's take a look at some transactions where my students have turned negative gearing problems into positive cash flow solutions in just a few weeks:

David – long-distance investment turnaround

The investor had a negatively geared property and needed cash flow relief. We agreed to put a rent-to-own buyer in the home and split the positive cash flow and profits if it sold for more than $230,000. The property was in Cairns, I was in Brisbane, and the investor was in country Queensland, so this was a long distance transaction!

I put an ad in the local newspaper, and I phoned the local supermarket, faxed a flyer through, and asked them to stick it on the community noticeboard out the front.

Then I spoke to the existing tenant, who hated the agent and the owner because they had been late making repairs after a cyclone a while back. I got the tenant a referral and helped

---

them to find a new place and get released from their 'terrible' lease. In return they showed people through the property for me, all at one convenient time.

In just a couple of weeks we found a suitable buyer, who bought the place for $300,000, and paid a $3,000 option fee and $500 a week for two years. Ironically, the agent had knocked this buyer back as a tenant just six months earlier, because they owned dogs. I never even saw the house until I flew up for the day to get all the paperwork signed – I completed the paperwork, had a swim and flew home for dinner.

Up-front deposit: $3,000 cash deposit

Cash flow: Rent of $500 a week, minus loan and outgoings of $330 a week, giving me a positive cash flow of $170 a week

Backend profit: $70,000

Geoff – car deposit turnaround

Another investor found me through word of mouth from an investors group. He had a property and wanted to turn his negative cash flow positive. We agreed to put a rent-to-own buyer in the house and split the profits over $250,000.

The buyers found me after just a few days from a newspaper ad for the property. This couple rang up and viewed the home on Saturday morning, then signed the paperwork and had the keys to the house on Saturday afternoon. They bought the place on a two-year lease option for $300,000 at $550 a week.

The buyers were talking about selling their second car to get the money for a deposit, so I suggested (for speed and convenience) that they just give me the car. They signed the car transfer papers as well as the lease option papers all in one meeting and moved in that day.

Up-front deposit: Car (I got $3,000 cash for the car from a wrecker on Monday morning)

Cash flow: Rent of $550 a week, minus loan and outgoings of $410 a week, giving me a positive cash flow of $140 a week

Backend profit: $50,000

A typical rent-to-own sign

Sandwich lease

(OR BACK-TO-BACK)

Finally, this is how you buy a house for a dollar! When you buy on a lease option, you only need a dollar to make the paperwork stick.

We had been using this strategy for over ten years when we read the book *McDonald's: Behind the Arches* by John F Love, and we learnt that the McDonald's Corporation used it to start its empire with almost no money down. The sandwich lease (also known as a back-to-back lease option) is probably one of the most flexible property strategies out there.

'We are not basically in the food business. We are in the real estate business. The only reason we sell fifteen-cent hamburgers is because they are the greatest producer of revenue from which our tenants can pay us our rent.'[1]

When McDonald's started franchising in the United States back in the late 1950s, it wasn't making any money from selling hamburgers. So using lease options, McDonald's bought up all the corner houses it could. It then subleased the properties to franchisees, and marked up the lease costs, first by 20% and then by 40%. So a store that cost McDonald's $600 per month would be charged out to the franchisee at a minimum of $840 per month.

'The beauty of McDonald's taking a 'sandwich' position on real estate – leasing from the property owner and subleasing to the franchisee – was that it produced predictable profit.'[2]

Then the company took things a step further and started to focus on property ownership.

'McDonald's was getting ownership of land and building without using any of its own money. It used the franchisees' money for down payments, and it borrowed the rest from landowners and banks ... [Sonneborn's] talents at financial negotiations and his keen appreciation for the interests of all parties to a deal could have been applied in any business, and Sonneborn would have been as content to apply them in the clothing business – his initial field – as in the hamburger business. In fact, he viewed the food service business merely as a vehicle for making money in real estate ... The name of the game was to make profit.'[3]

By using two lease options back-to-back, you can give this opportunity of home ownership to your tenants, just like McDonald's did with its franchisees, and *they* can rent before *they* buy. So you become the 'Transaction Engineer' and buy a property as an investor on a lease option, then you onsell the property to an end buyer on another lease option at a slightly higher price. And you make sure that you're receiving more money than you're paying so the transaction generates cash flow each month.

The sale price is agreed at the start of the transaction, and you effectively sublet the property to the buyer at a higher price than you're paying the seller. This way you get to profit from the sale of the property without ever officially owning it.

Here's how it works:

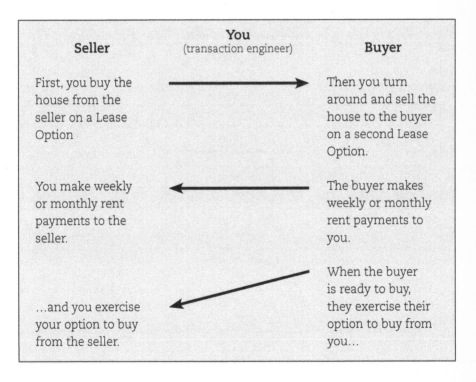

Seller	You (transaction engineer)	Buyer
First, you buy the house from the seller on a Lease Option	→	Then you turn around and sell the house to the buyer on a second Lease Option.
You make weekly or monthly rent payments to the seller.	←	The buyer makes weekly or monthly rent payments to you.
...and you exercise your option to buy from the seller.	←	When the buyer is ready to buy, they exercise their option to buy from you...

You can have total flexibility using back-to-back lease options.

Many times when we babysit sellers' loans we do it by using a rent-to-own paperwork system where the option to buy is simply the outstanding balance of the seller's loan at the time we wish to exercise the option to buy.

For example, if I babysit a seller's loan of $500,000, payable at a rate of 7% interest over 30 years, whatever the balance of the loan is when I decide to buy is the option price I pay.

If a price credit of X dollars per week is agreed to in the lease option to the buyer, the accumulated price credit comes off the price of the property if and when the person eventually buys. The price credit is the amount that goes on the option document.

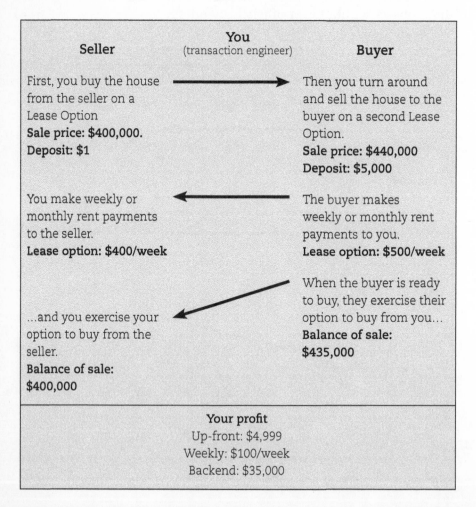

You
(transaction engineer)

Seller		**Buyer**
First, you buy the house from the seller on a Lease Option **Sale price: $400,000. Deposit: $1**	⟶	Then you turn around and sell the house to the buyer on a second Lease Option. **Sale price: $440,000 Deposit: $5,000**
You make weekly or monthly rent payments to the seller. **Lease option: $400/week**	⟵	The buyer makes weekly or monthly rent payments to you. **Lease option: $500/week**
...and you exercise your option to buy from the seller. **Balance of sale: $400,000**	⟵	When the buyer is ready to buy, they exercise their option to buy from you... **Balance of sale: $435,000**

Your profit
Up-front: $4,999
Weekly: $100/week
Backend: $35,000

Lease options are the most flexible of all the creative strategies we've talked about, and there are countless ways you can use them. You can use lease options in combination with pretty much every kind of strategy. Back-to-back lease options enable you to build up a portfolio of properties, so you can benefit from positive monthly cash flow capital-gain profits without taking on the usual fees and obligations of ownership.

Here are some more examples from my students that you may find interesting.

Brett – Gold Coast in three days

A couple in Lower Beachmont on the Gold Coast, QLD, had been trying to sell their house for over six months. They had already dropped the price a fair bit. They were motivated to sell, and found me through my website. We met at a local coffee shop on Saturday morning. Instead of keeping the house empty, I suggested, 'How about I give you your current asking price. Would you be happy if I looked after the loan payments until I'm in a position to go through with buying it?' They jumped at that idea, because the house had been vacant and eating a hole in their pocket for so long. Their asking price was $370,000. I started paying them $575 a week straightaway on a lease option, with two years to get the finance together.

I knew I had a buyer to onsell this property to, as I already had someone looking in the area. In fact, this couple had even looked at a house in the same street. They were very keen and although they were both on very good incomes, and had a reasonable deposit, it wasn't good enough for the bank. The lady was self-employed, so they could only go on the husband's income. I knew this house would suit them. I made a phone call and explained that I might have a house for them. They drove by the place on Sunday and got excited. We met on Monday and I gave them the keys.

I onsold the place to this couple. They paid a $15,000 deposit up-front and $855 a week, with the option to buy it at $418,000 in two years. They refinanced just three months later. This was the perfect stepping stone they needed to get into their first home. Houses in their street are easily worth $450,000. After they moved in, they were so grateful they invited us around for dinner. They put on an amazing feast, with a three-tiered platter of seafood, and cut-out pineapples and *piña coladas*. I got a call from them the other day. They still love it!

Up-front deposit: $15,000 cash deposit
Cash flow: Rent of $855 a week, minus loan and outgoings of $575 a week, giving me a positive cash flow of $290 a week
Backend profit: $33,000

Sirah – little pink house

This was a little pink house in a small suburb about an hour and a quarter outside of the city near Adelaide. The owners were a couple who wanted to move interstate to start their own business. They had renovated the bathroom, and had plans for new carpets, a new stove, and improvements to the garage and the gate. They wanted to move quickly and we agreed that they would finish their list of renovations before I took the house on for $216,000.

At the last minute the couple got called to move interstate sooner than they had planned. They didn't have the money to move immediately, but it was a big opportunity for their business and they didn't want to miss it. They asked me for the $4,000 they needed for moving expenses, and we agreed to simply take it off the price of the house. So we took the sale price down to $212,000, which was the total of their loan. I looked after their loan of just over $212,000, and they got to move on to start their own business interstate.

I sold the property by using a little paper sign in the local IGA community notice board. A lady saw the sign and told her daughter about it. The daughter and her partner had seven kids, and thought they'd never be able to own a home. I went through their details and saw that they could afford the payments on a two-year rent-to-buy for $270,000. They got started with a $5,000 deposit, and they were over the moon to have the opportunity to own their own home. They pay me $800 per fortnight, and I pay the owner $570 per fortnight.

Up-front deposit: $5,000

Cash flow: Rent of $800 a fortnight, minus outgoings of $570 a fortnight, giving me a positive cash flow of $230 a fortnight

Backend profit: $53,000

Rob – positive cash flow without ownership

I just did this transaction today. Some of the local real estate agents know to bring me properties that need to move fast. So an agent called me and said that this guy really needed to sell. He first listed at $270,000 and had dropped the price to $225,000. I offered $210,000, which he refused. I said I'd pay $225,000 if the seller paid the $5,000 commission to the agent. I pay $300 a week on a two-year lease option.

I onsold it to a new tenant/buyer on a lease option for $250,000, at $430 a week. It's not a bad weekly cash flow, and I've got no loan debt and no fees. The old owner pays for insurances and rates, and the new owner takes care of the house.

Up-front deposit: $8,000 cash deposit

Cash flow: I pay $300 a week and I receive $430 a week, giving me a positive cash flow of $130 a week

Backend profit: $25,000

Brett – sandwich lease in an hour

The buyer and the seller both found me via referral.

At 11 am I met the seller. He was absolutely stuck – he had already moved out, and was renting somewhere else. Then the sale of his property fell over, and he was stuck making payments on two places. He was asking $340,000. I bought the property on a lease option at that price and paid $640 a week, with $50 a week credited to the sale price, and I agreed to pay one mortgage payment.

At 12 pm I met the buyer. He had a decent income, but didn't have enough of a deposit to buy in the traditional way. He scraped together $10,000 for a deposit and I onsold the property to him on a lease option for $385,000 at $725 a week. Win/win/win!

Up-front deposit: $10,000 cash deposit

Cash flow: I pay $640 a week, and I receive $725 a week, giving me a positive cash flow of $85 a week

Backend profit: $35,000

References

1. John F Love, *McDonald's: behind the arches*, rev ed. Bantam Books, USA, 1995, p. 199.
2. ibid., p. 154.
3. ibid., pp. 155-156.

DOWNLOAD YOUR FREE FIVE INNOVATIVE PROPERTY STRATEGIES CHEAT SHEET

(Value $29.95 – yours FREE)

As my gift to you, download your **FREE 'Cheat Sheet' of my Five Innovative Property Strategies**. This is an easy summary of the five main strategies my students and I use every day.

Download your **FREE** copy at:

www.howtobuyahouseforadollar.com/free-stuff

So, where to now?

magine *now* buying your house for one dollar!

Imagine *now* buying your house without a bank.

Imagine *now* buying your home using none of your own money.

Imagine *now* buying a house even with less-than-perfect credit ...

... without paying stamp duty.

... without borrowing equity from your existing property.

... without saving for a deposit!

Imagine **now** how it empowering it will feel!

Having read this book, you know it's possible to buy as many houses as you want, using little or none of your own money and without getting a bank loan (even if you have less-than-perfect credit or have been locked out of the traditional banking system).

You've seen how to sell houses quickly, within a week or less, and get access to the cash locked up in the houses without delay.

Finally, you've experienced real-life stories and seen how positively uplifting it is to solve seemingly unsolvable financial problems simply by transferring houses from people who no longer want them to the people who do.

I sincerely hope that you have enjoyed reading this book. The next step is to put what you've discovered within these pages into action. Let's keep that momentum going! When I decided to write this book my objective was to share with you some of the incredible learning and insights I've gained over the years I've spent investing in property since 1991. Now, I want you to profit from what you're learning – and here's how you can: *by taking action.*

While I have outlined the basic principles, I've only just scratched the surface of what is possible using these strategies, as I have tried to keep the explanations simple and easy to understand. This path is perfect for anyone who is interested in buying their first property, turning a negatively geared property investment into a positive one, or creating positive cash flow.

Use this chapter as a catalyst to propel you to the next level. And as you move forward, ask yourself the following questions:

Who are you getting your advice from? If you're not getting your advice from millionaires, then is their advice worth the cost?

I believe that working with a mentor helps you to accelerate results in whichever area of life you intend to improve. It is far more efficient than trial and error.

When you're evaluating a mentor make sure that they're the right one for you. It's important that they are both an expert in their field *and* an exceptional trainer and coach who can successfully transfer their knowledge to you. You want to make sure they're not just an entertaining storyteller, but that they can convey information in a way that actually helps people to take action and get the same results that they did – or better.

Anyone can teach you property strategies and how the paperwork works. We teach people how to apply the strategies and get started. That's a big difference. It's the difference between knowing how it works, and relying on your day job until you can live life on your terms thanks to the income that your newly acquired specialised knowledge provides.

Judge your mentor by their own results, and, more importantly, by the results of their students.

Use a checklist to find the right mentor

The first step to success is finding a great mentor, and making sure they have a successful track record of helping people get the kind of results you want to get, at the level that you aspire to. Find out:

- What results they have achieved personally?
- How many years of experience they have in their field?
- How many years of experience they have had training students?
- What results their students have achieved?

In a perfect world I'd love to download all my knowledge, skills and experience that I've accumulated over 20 years into your head.

To get the most value from a great mentor, you need to become a great student. That means you need to start with an open mind, allow yourself to feel the power of pure possibility, and be willing to let your mentor guide you.

NOW, LET'S HEAR FROM SOME OF MY ADVANCED MENTORING STUDENTS

S Becker

I've been mentored by Rick for a few years now, and I still learn new things every time I talk to him.

I love the freedom and the money I get from this business.

It buys me lots of holidays. I take a solid two to three months off every year. Before I started doing this I was making a good income in IT, but I'm making four or five times that now. My partner and I have our dream farm now, and it's only been three years since I started working with Rick.

For anyone starting out, I think the most valuable thing is to learn and absorb as much as you can. I have Rick's audios on my iPhone and in my car. I still listen to Rick in the car. I can hear the same audio program 20 times, but I'm always able to pick up something new.

The thing I love about this business is that if you don't give up, you can't really fail. Even if you completely mess something up, it just means you make less profit.

In my first year I did about one house every four to six months. In my second year I did about one house a month. I'm doing about one house a week at the moment, and I've done about 100 altogether.

W & J Dugan

Rick's system works and makes money. It's a different way of buying and selling real estate. We suggest that if you pick one of Rick's tools and use it for one year, you'll become an expert. When you're done, go back and pick another tool and use that. It's like a horse race – you just put your blinkers on and go for it!

We love what we do. Our goal was to do five properties a year, with $70,000 profit in each property and do it for five years. We actually saw our results sooner than five years, and we are so pleased with them that we wouldn't do anything differently. It's amazing, how the $70,000 will fall from the tree, just when we need it.

John and I wanted a passive income, we wanted to be asleep and have money drop into our bank account, and by using Rick's systems, we do!

B Chislet

I met Rick when I went to listen to a share market speaker, and walked out using his strategies to do property. The most important thing I've learnt from Rick is to shift my headspace.

The most common question I get asked is how to get started. I started putting ads in papers to attract buyers and sellers and then put them together. I found just being out there talking to people creates opportunities. I love finding a way for all of us to work together by asking: is there another way?

I don't do this just for the money. I like what the money can do for me, but it also allows me to be who I really am and live the life I want for my three sons and my wife.

It's a liberating experience to do these strategies. I've made a lot more money doing Rick's strategies than I ever made in my old job.

I like doing a $30,000 transaction and having fun with it!

J & B Campbell-Bruce

Rick took us under his wing. He showed us the ropes to a life where we have hope and meaning, and I have my wife with me doing this, which is great. I am a schoolteacher, and have looked after 260 kids on my own. I needed to do something different. I wanted to do something that helps others, and at the same time provide for my family. This business has given us that opportunity. We have a life where we can do as much or as little work as we want to. We can give back, too. Soon we're going to be sponsoring orphanages in Thailand and we look forward to that. We're eternally thankful for what you've created.

S & M Donaldson

I remember when I first met Rick, I just wished that I knew all of the things he did and had all that experience! What inspires me about Rick's system is how good it feels to help buyers and sellers achieve their dreams.

I moved here from England, and had to do something to provide for my four kids, who were all under the age of seven. I wanted a work/ life balance and I have achieved that. Now, I'm one of the few dads who picks his kids up from school.

You don't need a lot of money to get started.

I've been doing property for four years full-time. I do about three transactions a month. It makes plenty of money and it's the life I've always wanted.

J & S Sarai

We moved here from Eastern Europe about ten years ago, and while English was not our first language we adapted to our new country and believed we were living the 'Aussie dream'.

We found with both of us working that we didn't get to see much of our son growing up as he was always in childcare. Even during school holidays we couldn't get time off work to be with him. We were working eight hours a day, and he was in care ten hours a day; it made us sad.

At the same time we had two negatively geared units on the Gold Coast. They were beautiful but every time we received a bill they became less attractive. It felt like all we were doing was working to support ourselves and our negatively geared properties.

When we met Rick and learnt his strategies, we sold our units to create positive cash flow. Next, our goal was to spend more time with our son and we did this by creating enough positive cash flow to replace our jobs. We have achieved that and more – my wife left her job in accounting and I left IT.

Now, we spend lots of time with our son, we travel together to Europe, the USA and the Pacific and we live in a beautiful house with a swimming pool in a nice suburb.

As you can see, my students were motivated to give my systems a go for various reasons. Some started working with me because they had lost their job, or they simply disliked what they were currently doing; others had a negatively geared property or needed passive income. But what they all had in common was they were open to new possibilities. For some of you, you may have to pretend to put all your money in a heap and burn it so you can feel what it's like to challenge yourself to be creative and look at property investing differently!

My students will tell you there are more than enough transactions for everyone, and how much they enjoy connecting with a group of like-minded people, focused on creating positive outcomes in property and in life.

For me, and many of our students, the opportunity to help solve the seemingly unsolvable property problems that currently exist today is what motivates us. It is an amazing, exhilaratingly positive feeling to help sellers avoid the pain of bankruptcy and to help buyers realise their dream of home ownership.

It **is** possible to become a property entrepreneur even if you've never bought or sold a house in your life. And it's possible for both the buyer and the seller to get what they want at the same time. It's not only possible, thousands of people from all walks of life have been doing it for years. And if they can do it, you can do it too.

As I related at the start of this book, when we were newly married and living in Dallas, my wife gave me 12 months to find a way to make my dreams a reality or get a nine-to-five job doing something that I wasn't passionate about. I discovered that when my back was against the wall, the only available space to move was *forward*.

I believe what I've laid out for you can be done intelligently, reasonably, intentionally, systematically and with passion. A common trait I've observed among the wealthiest people profiled in numerous books and business magazines is that they pursued their dream because they loved it and believed in it passionately. When you love something, you do it more often and you get better at it until, as 'the master of your craft', you have something everyone wants and they will pay for the best. Allow passion to be what drives you!

Recently I was training to run in Sydney's City2Surf, a 14-kilometre run stretching from the city to Bondi Beach. I told my trainer I could only run about eight kilometres. He told me to run in it anyway. He said the combined energy of all of us focusing on one goal – reaching the finish line – would be the catalyst to propel us forward. I knew my trainer was right, and even when I was tired, the momentum created by being part of the group picked me up and kept me going. We all ran as one towards our common goal, it felt exhilarating and empowering to be part of the group, breaking through our own barriers to finish the race!

I've shown you how you can buy your first home, grow your wealth with property and solve your property problems, without the headaches and hassles that have become so commonplace for most Australians and New Zealanders. And the best bit is that you don't need a lot of money or a bank loan to start using these strategies – just the willingness to see things a little differently.

Now is the time to move forward. Join us. My students and I welcome you. Make today the day you start putting your knowledge into action and changing not just your life, but the lives of many, many people who would otherwise not be able to enter the property market. Visit **www.howtobuyahouseforadollar.com/free-dvd** and we'll show you how to get started immediately!

What People Are Saying About Rick Otton

"Rick I just wanted to tell you I had a funny thing that happened three weeks ago. My work made me redundant! The funny part of it was that the night I got made redundant I signed up a seller and buyer to a deal that will make me my entire year's work salary – this transaction will net me $78,000! Let's just say I'm not taking any of the job offers that have come in since. I've already done two more deals in the last two weeks."
S Becker, Former IT Consultant, Victoria

"I got a call from sellers who were nine months behind on arrears and they were going to get evicted on 2 August and they gave me a call on 20 July. I sat down with them. They didn't want to leave and the bank was kicking them out. So we ended up buying that house off them and solving the problem with the arrears. Then sold to a family who was looking at doing the home up. The benefits to the vendors were they got to walk away with all of their debts paid and without their credit being shot. The benefits to the buyers are that they have a house. The benefits to my wife and I – we got $15,000 up-front, cash flow of $651 per month and backend we got around $27,000."
J Campbell-Bruce, Teacher, New South Wales

"I bought a property for $1.00. I made $10,000 up-front deposit, $440 per month positive cash flow and my backend profit is $27,000 ... Learning Rick's strategies I developed skills, now I know where I'm going and why I'm doing it and how I'm going to get there."
M Kelly, Former Developer, Queensland

"I had plans to become financially independent within five years, but through Rick's strategies I was able to do it within one year. Some of the other presenters' theories are great, but when you really go out to practice what they have taught, I have found I usually hit a brick wall; I can now not work as a doctor and do this full-time. The cash flow from my properties can now support pretty much my income. I still practice part-time as a doctor now, because I want to, not because I have to."
Dr G Ku, Doctor, Victoria

"Rick, we have today exchanged contracts on a $1.3 million house on a lease option for ourselves to live in, $15,000 up-front and $1,125 per week. Debt is $300,000 only. We are extremely grateful because this would not be possible without you! Expect our invite for a house-warming party."
J & S Sarai, IT Consultant & Bookkeeper, New South Wales

"We've been doing Rick Otton's strategies for the last 12 months. We've done nine transactions. Recently, we had a seller who was a burnt-out landlord who wanted to get away from his investment property. We had an investor who was a single mum with four kids and she had never invested before so we put the transaction together and made $11,000 in five hours. Our buyers had been on our database for nine months and when we met up with them they signed up straightaway. We've been invited (by them) for cocktails in their new home!"
B Clarke & K Mikina, Tradesman & Nurse, Victoria

"I've been working the whole of my life and I have created a property portfolio, but I had been working like 10, 15 hours a day to build what I had, and I did not see my children at all. I then retired and I had nothing to do. I came across your program and even at the age that I am, I decided to do it. Now while I am doing the program, I find that I am spending more time with my boys that are grown up and I'm enjoying having that drink with them, going out with them, and I'm a different person altogether. You have actually changed my life."
J Soulos, Retired Solicitor, New South Wales

"Here's my 'one-hour sandwich lease': I had a seller call me yesterday and after two minutes on the phone I agreed to meet at the house. I signed it up at 10:30 this morning. By lunchtime, I'd signed a buyer up, got a deposit and handed over the keys – AND got an invite back for a BBQ! That's an hourly rate of about $12,000! Love this business!"
B Mudie, Former IT Consultant, Queensland

"We have been using Rick Otton's rent-to-own system for the past 12 months or so. We had a bit of a slow start whilst we got the hang of using the rent-to-own system. But now we're blown away with the potential of the system. As a train driver I had to work a whole year to earn $64,000. With the rent-to-own system we earned in five weeks what would take me nearly two years to earn in wages as a train driver. We got $43,000 up-front in the bank and $93,000 equity, which we get later."
D & J Siacci, Former Train Driver and Housewife, Victoria

"We've made OVER $100,000 easily! What can I say ... anyone who can take the subject of real estate investing and inform and entertain at the same time is extraordinary!"
J Muir & J Elliot, Consultants, New South Wales

"I'm Wayne from Victoria and the deal I did recently was done remotely in Queensland. I put a transaction together for a group of sellers who were a bit troubled by making their repayments. The house sold for $305,000 (the agents couldn't sell it for $287,000). I got in buyers, a truck-driver husband and a nurse wife. They had had trouble with some credit reports in the past, and it was an opportunity for them to get in and own their own home now. I made $20,000."
W Revell, IT, Victoria

"Rick's knowledge is the best ... and he delivers it so everybody can understand it easily. Rick's systems work perfectly. Thanks for all your knowledge and support. In appreciation."
M Kelly, Buyer's Agent, New South Wales

"I used to work at Woolworths driving forklifts for about eight years. I came to Rick's bootcamp 18 months ago – and around that time my third son was born. I haven't worked a day since then. I was earning $43,000 a year – I actually made more than that last week. My first backend cheque was $47,000! As a forklift driver I never answered the phone or had any customer interaction at all."
J Monoghan, Former Forklift Driver, South Australia

"We bought a property without a bank loan, we made $10,000 up-front deposit, $800 per month positive cash flow and our backend profit is $70,000."
S & M Donaldson, Small Business Owners, Queensland

"I am over the moon. I just got the last bits of our first deal done – and the new owners couldn't stop thanking us for giving them this opportunity to own their own home! I found that enormously satisfying. Thanks to you, Rick, and the We Buy Houses team. Thanks for opening the concepts to us in a way that we could put into action. We can't wait to get our next deal done and our new property business snowballing along!"
J Lloyd, Western Australia

"Thanks Rick, it has not even been a full week since I have left your course and your strategies have helped me make $10,000, and it doesn't stop there. The rest of the deal looks something like this: $624 cash flow per month, $63,000 backend profit (roughly). Not bad for a property that was just neutrally geared less than a week ago."
H Broughton, Queensland

"Hi Rick, we completed our first sandwich lease option, we received $7,000 up-front, $120 per week positive cash flow and a backend profit of $32,520. Thank you so much for your help and direction."
R Archdall, Cleaning Company Owner, Western Australia

"On a recent transaction I received $10,000 up-front and my backend profit was $30,156.38. One of the biggest things I learnt from Rick is it doesn't matter what happens in the world – if I lost everything I owned right now I know I'm going to be okay. Because I know that I have the skill set to go and do it all again and I am going to have a lot of fun and I'm going to help a lot of people doing this at the same time."
T Hart, Former Bank Worker, Victoria

"I've been around real estate for a fair while as a developer. Rick has taught me a lot more about negotiating and how to fix problems. Now I'm able to go out and fix other people's problems, which has also created a great income for myself."
G Thomas, Former Developer, New South Wales

"We recently just helped a lady who lost her job and couldn't afford the mortgage payments. We found a buyer who had problems getting a bank loan because of his past credit history. We put the buyer and seller together. She got rid of her problem. He got the house for his family. We made $40,000 in the deal, everyone is happy and it is a win-win situation."
A & C Chua, Franchise Owners, Western Australia

"Just bought my first place for $1.00 and sold my other property on a lease option for $30,000 more than what the agent could get me. All smiles."
C Eckert, New South Wales

"Exciting news ... just closed another sandwich deal. Deposit from buyers included a car. Good profit on deal with no money down from us ... this is fun! Great teamwork – I'm sourcing sandwich properties and Alex is selling them. Business is growing from strength to strength."
G & A Close, Queensland

"Just sharing some great news ... We sold three of our houses in one week! Actual time spent by Monique and I, including show through, placing ads, putting up signs etc ... 22 hours. Thanks Rick for your wisdom ..."
P & M Verbaten, Former Chemist & Housewife, Victoria

"My brother and I received $18,000 up-front in cash and our backend profit is $162,000 from two transactions. We invested no money and did not qualify for any bank loans."
P Grimaldi, Telecommunications Serviceman, New South Wales

"We have completed five properties. They are generating a positive cash flow in excess of $100 per week per property, $650 per week cash positive to date. We have locked in profits from $30,000 to $50,000 per property. Our capital gain is in the order of $220,000. We had attended an American seminar but it didn't provide the necessary nitty-gritty details to make it happen. Rick's system filled in the gaps."
J & W Dugan, Property Developer & Jewellery Designer, Queensland

"I went to Rick Otton's bootcamp for three days, I spent $2.00 and I bought two houses and I made $17,000 cash and $72,000 backend profit ... and I have a skill going as well. Thank you very much for that."
T Cat, New South Wales

"I've been in property for the last 10 years. I had a number of negatively geared properties and since doing Rick's strategies, I've been able to turn those properties around and they now provide positive cash flow. I did one deal using Rick's system and I wasn't sure how I was going to pay for it, so I put the deposit on a number of credit cards and I managed to negotiate a 12-month settlement. Long story short, it's going to cost me interest on the deposit for 12 months, and since the day that I bought the property, the property has gone up $200,000 and I'm about to cash out of that deal. It cost me $12,000 and I'm going to make $200,000. One of my goals was to purchase a Jaguar (car) because my father died when I was seven and one of his goals was to buy a Jag and I'm fulfilling his dream. So 47 years later ... I've dreamed of that for 47 years and Rick has enabled me to do that."
R Holt, Victoria

"We made $740,000 in 10 months from one transaction."
S & S Carr, New Zealand

"We bought our first house for $50 and we've got $30,000 in the deal. We're getting $70 a week cash flow out of it and it will settle in 18 months, the people are ecstatic and we're ecstatic, the people who sold it are happy and the people who bought it are more than happy."
W & D Bamber, Small Business Owners, New South Wales

GLOSSARY

Deposit finance – also known as 'second mortgage carry back', this is where the buyer gets a bank loan for as much as they can borrow, and the seller lends them what they can't borrow and takes on a second mortgage security. The buyer then passes the loan over time in monthly payments with interest, or in a lump sum.

Handyman special – a strategy used to buy or sell a property that needs cosmetic work; the buyer's 'sweat' equity becomes the deposit for the property.

Instalment contracts – known as 'instalment sales' or 'terms contracts', these have been around for over 100 years in Australia. The seller provides the buyer with a principal and interest loan for 25–30 years and the buyer pays monthly instalments to the seller.

Negative gearing – this is where the money coming in is less than the money going out every month on an investment property, and the monthly shortfall can be claimed as a loss on your tax return. High-income earners use this to reduce their taxable income. Various vendor finance strategies can turn negatively geared property cash flow neutral or positive.

Off the plan – when you buy 'off the plan' you are buying a property before it's built.

Positive cash flow – also known as 'positive gearing', this is when more money is coming in than going out every month on a property after costs. During each month money is received in the form of rent-to-own or instalment contract payments. There are various vendor finance strategies that can create positive cash flow.

Rent-to-own – also known as a 'rent-to-buy', 'rent-now-buy-later', 'rent purchase agreement' or 'lease option', this means the buyer leases the property for an agreed amount of time, for an agreed price up-front. At the same time, the buyer has the option but not the obligation to purchase the property.

Sandwich lease option – also known as a 'back-to-back lease option', or 'how to buy a house for a dollar', as the middle man you buy a property from a seller on a lease option and then onsell the property to an end buyer on a separate lease option at a slightly higher price. The sales price and terms for both lease options are agreed upon up-front. The person in the middle putting the agreement and legal paperwork together is called the transaction engineer.

Stamp duty – a state government tax on the transfer of property, calculated on the value of the property. The amount of stamp duty applicable varies by sale price and by state.

Upside down loan – this is where more debt is owed on a property than it's worth. In this situation, if a seller tried to sell the traditional way through a real estate agent, they would need to bring money to settlement to satisfy the outstanding debt. Various vendor finance strategies can be used to turn an upside down loan around so that the seller doesn't need to bring money to the settlement table.

Vendor finance – also known as 'seller finance', this is where the seller offers easy payment terms to the buyer. So instead of the buyer paying the full price up-front, they can pay the property off. There are different kinds of paperwork that can support vendor finance transactions. Vendor finance was used starting over 100 years ago, and tends to increase in popularity when bank financing becomes more difficult to obtain. The various forms of vendor finance are known as 'terms contracts', 'vendors' terms', 'instalment contracts', 'instalment sales,' 'rent-to-own', 'rent-to-buy', 'rent-now-buy-later', 'rent purchase agreements', 'sandwich lease option', 'back-to-back lease option', 'how to buy a house for a dollar', 'deposit finance', and the 'handyman special'.